THE DELAWARE WING-T

AN ORDER OF FOOTBALL

H.R. "Tubby" Raymond
and
Ted Kempski

Parker Publishing Co., Inc.
West Nyack, NY

Third Printing . . . . . September 1987

DEDICATION

To the Delaware Football players, whose efforts led to the writing of this book.

Library of Congress Cataloging-in-Publication Data

Raymond, Harold R.
  The Delaware Wing-T.

  Bibliography: p.
  Includes index.
  1. Football—Offense. 2. Football—Coaching.
I. Kempski, Ted. II. Title.
GV951.8.R39   1986   796.332'2   86-12174

ISBN 0-13-198326-1

Printed in the United States of America

CONTENTS

PREFACE v

ACKNOLWEDGMENTS vii

WHAT THIS BOOK WILL SHOW YOU ix

I   THE DELAWARE FOOTBALL SYSTEM 1

    1   Delaware Football—A Rich Heritage   2

    2   A Psychology of Coaching   8

    3   Philosophy and Design of the Delaware Wing-T   19

II   THE DEFENSES 31

    4   A Study of Defenses   32

    5   Attacking the Defense   41

III   ELEMENTS OF THE OFFENSE 67

    6   Offensive Communication and Structure   68

    7   Offensive Summary   82

IV   COACHING POSITION TECHNIQUES 105

    8   The Quarterback   106

    9   The Running Backs   116

    10   The Linemen   133

    11   The Ends   148

V   ORGANIZATION FOR SUCCESS 165

    12   The Teaching Progression   166

    13   Perfect Practice Makes Perfect   171

    14   The Variables of Offensive Football   178

VI   THE PLAYS 189

    15   The Plays   190

    BIBLIOGRAPHY 231

    INDEX 237

PREFACE

This book is regarded, in some respects as a debt to be paid, for it passes to you, the reader, a legacy of a discipline of football that it has been my fortune to experience. People have often asked, "What is the single most influential factor of your coaching experience?" I have answered quickly; without question it has been the systematic "order of football" that was introduced to me at the University of Michigan some 30 years ago by the late Fritz Crisler, then football coach there. I'm certain it had its formation from Alonzo Stagg, who was Crisler's coach and has been a foundation of coaching success at virtually all levels of football. It was brought to fruition here at Delaware by Dave Nelson whom I have always considered my mentor. Benny Osterbaan, Forest Evashevski, Biggie Munn, Duffy Dougherty, Frank Kush, Chuck Fairbanks, Pete Elliot, Gerry Burns, Bob Hollway, Ara Parseghian, and Harold Westerman are just a few of the great football coaches who have used this discipline of football.

This "order of football" supersedes a formation, because it is a complete approach to the game. It begins with a numbering system that clearly communicates our offensive play and its assignments. It includes a design of offense that relates series and plays creating defensive conflicts. It spreads skill requirements of players so they can realize their greatest potential and gives your team the best chance of winning. In short, this book passes on to you a total system of offensive football. Its foundation enables you to check the soundness of your own ideas. I hope that this book will give you more than the numbers of a system, for the legacy to which I refer extends beyond Xs and Os.

The men who have passed this legacy to me have repeatedly shown a high regard for the men who play the game. They have demonstrated a respect for them as individuals, even though they are taking part in a very team-oriented game.

The player's welfare must precede that of the coach. The player must assume a position of importance and none of these great coaches I have mentioned, in spite of their fame, have ever been more important than the individuals who comprise their teams.

In this "order," the responsibility for winning or losing is clearly that of the players. If it were otherwise and the coach accepted this responsibility he would then be credited with all the thrill of winning and would usurp all the credit for the game itself.

This legacy which I pass to you finally shows a great regard for the game itself. It begins with respect for the rules of the game both in letter and in spirit. This respect extends to the safety of your players, the teaching of techniques that are not only sound from a football standpoint but have the players' safety in mind as well.

It is my opinion that football, properly coached, can make an exceptional contribution to the education of its players. Our communities can use the discipline of football—only your teaching will protect the game, its name, and the position it holds in our society.

It is with a great deal of pride that I pass to you the legacy of Delaware football and hope that it will make a contribution not only to you, but to your young men who play the game. (See the Bibliography for historical evolution.)

H.R.R.

ACKNOWLEDGMENTS

In writing this book, which is the summation of the evolution of an offensive system, we were reminded of all the coaches who contributed to the Delaware Offense. David M. Nelson, Gene Stauber, Milo R. Lude, Irvin C. Wisniewski, Raymond B. Duncan, Rocco Carzo, Edward F. Maley, Michael Heineken, James E. Flynn, James Grube, Chris Raymond, William "Herky" Billings, Ronald G. Rogerson, Gregg A. Perry, Robert F. Sabol, Theodore C. Kempski, Harold R. Raymond, as well as many other men who have coached the Wing-T at other institutions.

Credit must also be given to Cathy Combs, our tireless secretary, and Eve Kempski who typed this book.

WHAT THIS BOOK WILL SHOW YOU

The Delaware Wing-T: An Order of Football is an answer to all the inquiries received from coaches at every level, professional, college, high school, and junior high school, as well as coaches from Canada, Mexico, and Japan. Therefore, the Wing-T is presented in an orderly form to show how the University of Delaware has been able to consistently place among the National leaders offensively in scoring, total offense, and rushing offense during the past two decades.

In order to be successful, an offensive system must be versatile and, therefore, multiple. It must also be executed to near perfection so that success is directly related to how well the players learn details and understand the subtle intricacies within the system.

A major emphasis, therefore, has been placed on teaching the system. The organization of teaching is covered two ways. First, a psychology of coaching is presented to serve as a foundation for all that follows, as the Delaware Wing-T is in many ways an outgrowth of this psychology. Second, a progression is developed showing the order in which the systems should be introduced and the practice plan to ultimately carry out this order.

The Delaware Wing-T provides the reader with a thorough understanding of the system by discussing the philosophy and design, emphasizing its versatility, which includes the Lead Post Principle, Blocked Flanks, Option Flanks, Drop Back Passing, and the best Play-Action Passing in football. An analysis of the various defenses is also covered, including a graphic description of how to attack these defenses.

Individual coaching techniques are presented in three major areas:

    I. Line: Stance, Shoulder Block, Lead Post, Pass Protection

        A. Center—Snap

        B. Guard—Pull, Log, Wall Off

        C. Tackle—Trap

II. End: Receiving Skills

    A. Tight End—Releases

    B. Split End—Crack Block, Stalk Block

III. Backfield: Running Skills

    A. Quarterback—Stance, Pivot, Handoff, Fake, Pass

    B. Fullback—Stance, Handoff, Block

    C. Halfback

        1. Diveback—Stance, Handoff, Block

        2. Wingback—Stance, Block, Motion

Finally, the entire Delaware Playbook is included, covering the assignments, diagrams against the most popular defenses, individual coaching points, formation variations, and blocking adjustments.

The Delaware Wing-T will successfully show how to install and operate one of the most exciting and enjoyable offenses in football.

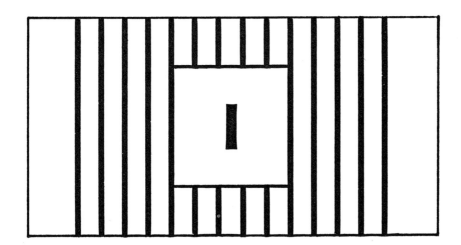

THE DELAWARE
FOOTBALL SYSTEM

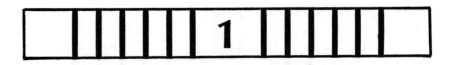

DELAWARE FOOTBALL—
A RICH HERITAGE

Delaware and the Fightin' Blue Hens have always been synonymous with winning in collegiate football circles.

In the early 1950s, Dave Nelson began one of the Nation's outstanding football dynasties. It was under Nelson that Delaware first gained national recognition as a football power. The "Admiral" directed teams to a win in the Refrigerator Bowl, three Middle Atlantic Conference Championships, Three Lambert Cups, and earned 1963 laurels as the nation's top collegiate division team. Nelson retired in 1966 and handed the reins to assistant Tubby Raymond.

From 1966 through 1984, Delaware teams have won three Middle Atlantic Championships, ten Lambert Cups, twelve Eastern Championships with wins in a Boardwalk Bowl in 1968, 1969, 1970, and 1971, and three National Championships. The 1968, 1970, 1971, and 1982 teams led the nation in rushing offense while the 1969, 1971, and 1979 teams were the total offense leaders. The 1973, 1974, 1976, 1978, 1979, 1981, and 1982 teams played in the tournament for the National Championship. The 1971 and 1972 teams were the unanimous choice as National Champions, while the 1979 team won the National Championship Playoffs. The 1976, 1978, 1979, 1981, and 1982 teams were selected as the ECAC Team of the Year for those years. The NCAA recently revealed that the University of Delaware football teams achieved the best win and loss percentages of all Division II teams in America during the period 1975-1980. In 1980, Delaware moved into NCAA Division 1-AA and responded quickly by being selected as the Eastern Division 1-AA Team of the Year in 1981 and 1982.

Forest Evashevski at Iowa, Ara Parseghian at Notre Dame, and Paul Dietzel at LSU also won National Championships while using the Wing-T.

2

Much of the success enjoyed at Delaware is attributable to the Wing-T offense, which was invented by Dave Nelson at Maine in 1950 and perfected at Delaware in the early 1950s. The original offense evolved from the Michigan Single Wing of Fritz Crisler and the Army Trap Series of Earl "Red" Blaik. Although the Wing formation was used by others prior to this, it was not developed into a complete offense. By combining the Single Wing and Trap series and adding a QB Bootleg, Nelson developed the Wing-T into a complete offense, which has endured defensive change for over three decades.

Because of this defensive change, which significantly increased in sophistication, many offenses became nearly obsolete. Examples of this are the Single Wing and the Split T. In order to avoid obsolescence, the Delaware Wing-T has naturally had to change and grow to remain a successful offensive force in modern football. The first significant development was the addition of a counter in the twenty series with the quarterback executing an inside handoff. Putting in the option added to the system's versatility at the flank, while the belly series served the same function internally. The addition of a spread receiver enhanced both the passing and flank games. Because of defensive pressure the addition of a "Gap" rule to each lineman's basic assignments was the most significant addition to line play. The use of "Gut" blocking, both up the middle and offtackle added finesse blocking to the scheme and the conditional post and bump lead were more important refinements to the original lead post. The conditional post was particuarly significant because it solved many of the gap problems off the backside. Important developments in the passing game include the addition of called patterns to play-action passes in which the quarterback pulls up providing a dropback effect. The use of double wing was also significant as was the addition of a flanker to the double wing set. The addition of the flanker led to more sophistication within the dropback scheme, particularly with combination and under patterns. Other significant developments are:

(1) 1951—121 (Figure 1-1) The first Wing-T sweep was taken directly from the single wing with the wingback blocking the outside man on the line of scrimmage and the tight end releasing inside and then blocking out.

1956—121 (Figure 1-2) Changes in defensive support angles forced an adjustment in the sweep blocking with both the wingback

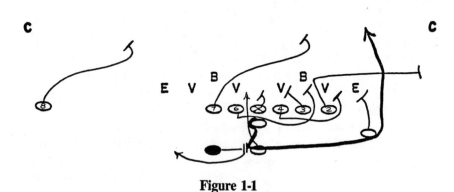

Figure 1-1

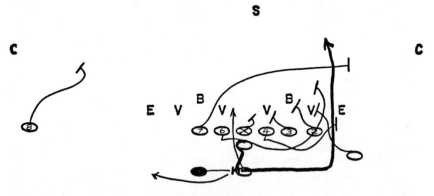

Figure 1-2

and tight end blocking the first man to the inside and the playside guard pulling and blocking out the support.

1964—129 (Figure 1-3) In order to maintain the mirrored approach to the offense, the blocking was adjusted so that the sweep could be run away from the wingback to the split end. This initiated the use of a split end to the attack.

(2) 1957—134 Counter (Figure 1-4) The addition of the tackle trap, which was introduced in 1955 and consummated in 1957 as 134 ct tackle pull, resulted in the development of the most classic of all Wing-T running plays. This play is still a foundation of the attack and is used by virtually every NFL team.

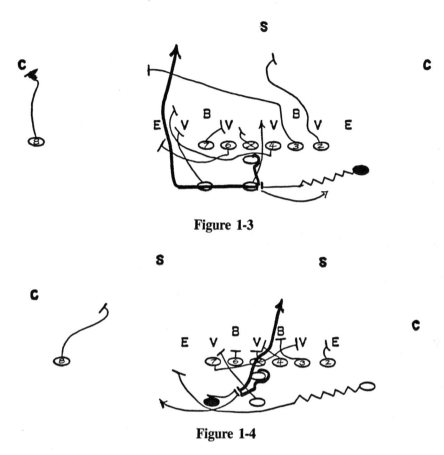

Figure 1-3

Figure 1-4

(3) 1959—187 Cross Block (Figure 1-5) The belly series was finalized with the addition of the cross block. This play has proven to be the most consistent running play in the offense.

(4) 1968—129 Waggle (Prior to this all waggles were from the 30 series) (Figure 1-6) The most significant development in the offense was the addition of the waggle with the quarterback faking the sweep to the left and keeping the ball to the right. Both guards go opposite the sweep action and block for the QB. The FB dives up the middle and goes into the weakside flat. The timing between the backside guard and the fullback was difficult and took a number of years to master.

(5) 1978—129 Trap Option (Figure 1-7) The Trap Option created two conflicts for the defense and initiated the use of the option in the

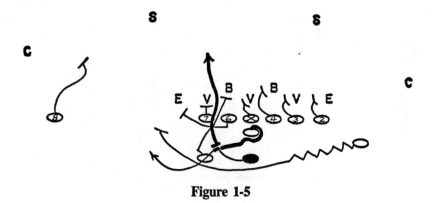

Figure 1-5

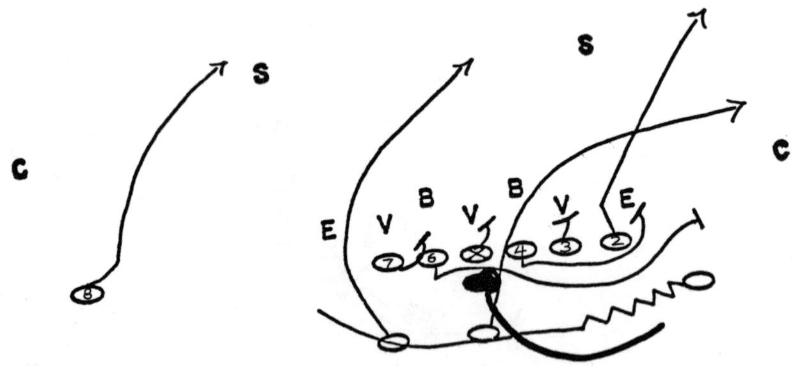

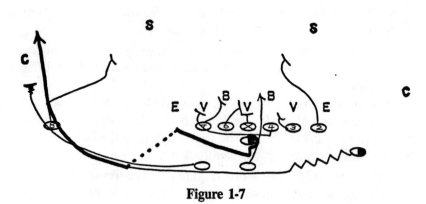

Figure 1-6

Figure 1-7

Wing-T attack. The blocking scheme gives the appearance of a Trap play up the middle while the backfield action resembles the Waggle (Figure 1-6).

(6) 1981—182 Down Option (Figure 1-8) The Belly option was developed coordinating the best off-tackle blocking scheme with the option.

(7) 1983—123 Guard Trap to Left Half (Figure 1-9) The addition of an inside handoff to the sweep series enables the running back to go inside giving the series a good off-tackle play to the HB.

Delaware football teams have become known as much for their spirit and determination as they are for faultless execution and technique. The combination has produced a winning tradition and rich heritage that is now being passed on to you.

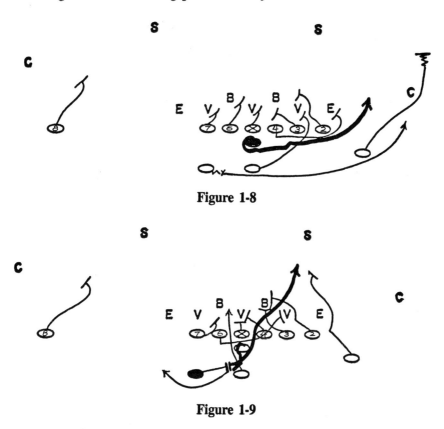

Figure 1-8

Figure 1-9

2

A PSYCHOLOGY OF COACHING

Every successful football coach is in some measure a psychologist! Not only is the practice of psychology an important territory in coaching, but it's an area where everyone can be an expert. Your psychological approach may be just as effective as anyone's, and has probably helped you win. No one, from Freud to Skinner, has been accepted by everyone. This is true for certain psychological principles that we believe have played a role in our success at Delaware. We would like to share not only our plays and formations, but our psychological stance as well.

Psychology is, of course, the study of human behavior, and anyone whose success demands teaching, directing, communicating, or interacting with people must certainly be aware of human behavior. We should recognize that everyone has needs to be fulfilled. Everyone has a series of goals, things he would like to be or things he would like to accomplish, even if these goals are subliminal. If you want to be successful with personal interactions, show people how they can fulfill their needs and work toward the accomplishment of their goals. If you are going to communicate with people, and that is a must in coaching, you must develop a genuine interest in their well-being.

Now let's be honest about it! Your interest in psychology is *motivation*. This is the technique that enables you as a coach to do something or say something that inspires those around you to deeds that would ordinarily be considered impossible. It's possible that no one can do that, and it is likely that those coaches who are considered especially adept at motivating peers and players have a knack for surrounding themselves with highly motivated people.

We must be careful about our approach to motivation. If someone feels you are trying to motivate him, he may resist. Motivation implies manipulation, and no one wants to be manipulated! No one wants his space invaded. People do not want to be made to do anything. They don't want to be made to laugh, to be sold, or to be motivated. Remember, everyone likes to be entertained and the happiest people are often those who have just bought something. But they have bought something and it is an exceptional treat when they feel they've consummated a *good deal!*

MOTIVATION

For the record, as long as we're talking about motivation, let's examine those things that cause us to move. There are only two, and they are very simple: positive and negative. Anticipation of reward, recognition, and accomplishment are positive stimuli. Fear of punishment, rejection, and failure are negative stimuli. When either reward or punishment are imminent, motivation to action is usually one of the reactions. A football coach, sensitive to the individual, can use one of these two extremes to encourage players to extend themselves.

The football coach assumes a tough assignment when he is asked to meet people's needs through the medium of a team sport. The first step is to demonstrate that personal goals can readily be sublimated for team-oriented goals, and that many of their wishes can be fulfilled by being a part of a successful team.

If you are constantly aware of the individual as you are developing your team, you will establish a thorough orientation program. Your team should know "why" before they ask. Everything should be discussed with team members before they become players. The general conduct rules should be explained, not as laws, but in terms of why they are necessary. For example, "I want you to be on time because it inconveniences your teammates when you are late, and that makes interaction within the team difficult." "You will be well conditioned because only a well-conditioned athlete is able to perform to his capabilities and excel on Saturday." "We want you to look good! Wouldn't you like to investigate the limits of your abilities?"

ORIENTATION PROGRAM

This orientation should begin with the objectives of football and why it is being supported by an educational institution. Here are examples of two summer letters that leave little to the imagination. The first is sent early in the summer and contains a commitment card that must be signed before preseason camp.

FIRST LETTER:

To the candidates of the DELAWARE FOOTBALL team:

This football team began with your winter conditioning program and progressed through spring practice. The summer, now, gives us a brief time to reflect upon our progress and determine what should be done to make your team a winner! It is extremely important that we take the time this summer to outline, through a summer letter project, the requirements of a winning team.

Although football is a highly organized game designed to tax intelligent men, there are few activities that place such an enormous premium on just sheer effort. We know that your "mental stance" is as important as your physical ability and want to begin by pointing out this incredibly important aspect of your team. I have seen men of modest ability become effective players simply because they placed football in high priority and thoroughly applied themselves.

This will be the first of several letters that you will receive this summer regarding what you can expect from DELAWARE FOOTBALL, and what will be expected from you. If this is your first year with us, read them carefully. Your understanding of them could make a difference! If you've been here before and feel you've heard it all, I urge you to read them again; we can't take anything for granted. Enlisting a total commitment requires a thorough understanding of our objectives, for no one can fully extend himself without knowing exactly what is expected and why.

DELAWARE FOOTBALL is designed as a phase of your education and is compatible with your studies. DELAWARE FOOTBALL is not a business or a way of life, but I hope you recognize that football can add an important dimension to your collegiate experience in addition to being highly rewarding and a great deal of fun. The course content of our program includes loyalty, discipline, and a physical test of your strength, endurance, and courage. It is an experience in sacrifice where you will be asked to sublimate personal goals for team objectives.

DELAWARE FOOTBALL represents a special opportunity for young men of your age. Your football experience will be a fleeting one, and I urge you to recognize that it is a once-in-a-lifetime opportunity before it eludes you. It is an unforgiving experience in that each game is played just once, and the results are invariably related to the extent of your effort in preparation and playing. The game is totally objective. It ignores the spoken word and cares only for what you do as it deals its rewards. It may require an adjustment of your priorities, but I would like to remind you that all of the things that conflict with football can be done repeatedly the rest of your life, but you have only one opportunity to experience DELAWARE FOOTBALL.

The nature of DELAWARE FOOTBALL requires one person's success to depend upon the effort of many. When you work with someone and depend on him, loyalty becomes a necessity. This means that we as coaches see that your best interests are served and that you, in turn, exhibit a concern for your teammates and coaches as well. No group effort can be successful without loyalty, and paradoxically, disloyalty demeans the individual more than it hurts the group. Our concept of loyalty extends beyond individuals and encompasses principles such as *accepting* the *discipline* of *training rules*. No team will become great with even a single dissident. Only complete loyalty will enable you to extend your effort beyond your limits and believe me, if we are going to continue our tradition, this will be necessary.

During the past few years, there has been evidence that there are fewer men who adhere to the letter of our training rules. It is also evident that living in university housing may not be conducive to training or any form of disciplined living. But that situation is "given" and requires more from your commitment to ignore the freedom that is apparent and to follow the rules of a demanding program. Our training rules are simple and without compromise. Those who play here will not use tobacco in any form, alcohol, or non-therapeutic drugs. If you're interested in a style of living that includes these as "highs" in your life—you are not a DELAWARE FOOTBALL PLAYER! When you accept the responsibility of DELAWARE FOOTBALL, you will recognize the rules that are necessary for the discipline of a well-trained team. Remember, the best prepared, most commited team has the best chance of winning. It requires that you accept the many meanings of the word discipline as applied to football. You recognize the discipline of individual assignments which makes the team concept of football possible and it enables you to continue to play successfully even though things may not be going well for you personally. Discipline creates beautiful music; it also enables a football team to win. It is only through this approach that we can stay together when things become difficult.

The first ingredient for an exceptional football team, now as in the past, will be that everyone enthusiastically join the team. You must join without reservation, recognizing team goals as well as your own. You must place football in high priority. DELAWARE FOOTBALL is no place for anyone with a casual interest. Certainly, I would want you to join for your own personal reasons, but I sincerely hope that if you become accountable for your team, its recognition and rewards will become personal. Accepting the responsibility of DELAWARE FOOTBALL is no small task, as we have become nationally known and a great deal is expected of you. The mantle of DELAWARE FOOTBALL is now placed on your shoulders; it is my hope that you will accept this responsibility with a great deal of pride, and enjoy the feeling of having made your team successful.

This is not an invitation to return for early practice, but an attempt to learn on whom we can depend this fall. If you understand what we need and can join, use the enclosed card to inform me of your intentions. (Figure 2-1) Accepting this responsibility commits you to a demanding three-week, preseason training camp, and sixty unforgiving minutes of a most difficult eleven-game schedule, regardless of the assignment given you. The period of investigation is over We need people who insist on success.

I have spoken often of the accomplishment of DELAWARE FOOTBALL with great pride, and again urge you to make a commitment to becoming an unselfish member of what could be a great football team. I look forward to hearing from you soon, and hope that you will join the DELAWARE FOOTBALL team—the most demanding, selective, and rewarding group on campus.

Yours for the responsibility of
DELAWARE FOOTBALL,

Harold R. Raymond
Head Coach of Football

I understand what will be expected of me this fall and I join the team without reservation, regardless of the assignment given me. I look forward to accepting a share of the responsibility for Delaware football.

_____ The team can count on me.

_____ I wish to eliminate myself from the team.

In addition, I agree that if I leave the camp for any reason other than medical I will pay my expenses at the rate of $25 per day because in leaving I have taken someone else's place.

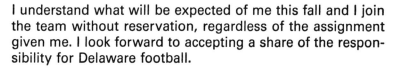

Signature

Figure 2-1

SECOND LETTER:

MEMO TO: MEMBERS OF THE UNIVERSITY OF DELAWARE FOOTBALL TEAM

This will be the last and most significant of your summer letters, for it is your invitation to join the DELAWARE FOOTBALL TEAM. It is an invitation to become a member of the most select group on campus and an opportunity to engage in a special project—creating a Delaware Championship Football Team. I invite you to join, yet insist that you fully understand the letters that have preceded this one—that you recognize the purpose of our program and the responsibility that you are accepting.

I would like to remind you once more that you are inheriting one of the finest football traditions in the country—our winning has been attributed to a number of reasons, but the basis of our success has been the quality of commitment made by a number of fine football players.

You have already indicated your willingness to join the team with the postcard you signed. I want you to know that your willingness to "come to play" is a decision of far greater importance than any we may make as coaches. We need your commitment and uncompromising effort to make this year a source of pride in which we can all share.

You must report to the Pencader Dining Hall @ 8:00 A.M. on August 21 for our initial team get-together. You will be given information about your physical exam and room assignment at this meeting.

I will look forward to seeing you and would like to extend the best wishes for your Football Team.

Yours in commitment,

Harold R. Raymond
Head Coach of Football

TEACH OWNERSHIP

The coach should give the team to the players through their leadership corps as soon as possible! Make it *their* team and not the coaches' team. This procedure begins by selling the *responsibility* for the success at the outset. You want them to assume the ownership of the group. You can say something like:

> I wasn't a very good football player when I was a kid, and now that I can't run, tackle, or catch the ball, it isn't likely that I'm going to be much help to you. Oh, I can give you plays and help you select who's going to play, (the coach should hang on to that responsibility) but when things are tough on the field you'll have to make a big play.

Now this may sound humorous to you, but it does make sense. The coach who assumes total control and ownership of the team robs his players of the one big reason they're playing. They want a measure of autonomy over their playing experiences. They need to feel that they have a real stake in the overall plan, and even the thrill of winning! If you're interested in this idea, then you can't take the blame for losing either. For example, "I was out-coached today," may sound like a generous statement today, but when you win the next week the implication is that today we won because of my coaching. A coach of a player-oriented team can never be greater than his players—it just doesn't work!

Establishing "ownership" for a player is one of your most effective psychological tasks. Demonstrating to them that it's their team, and that both the rewards and the embarrassment of failure will be theirs, is an important aspect of Delaware football. While young men may be asked to "die for their Alma Mater," they'd much rather live for themselves.

SELF ESTEEM

Try to create and strengthen each player's self esteem. Self esteem begins with a sense of autonomy. What he can be under certain conditions should be made clear. Having an open door for personal discussions about what he can do not only helps his own personal image, but lends insight into what he would like to be. Remember, the greatest single positive thing you can do as a coach is to help your players realize their needs and their potential. Help them get what they want!

Several years ago, we had a sophmore quarterback for whom we called all of the plays from the sideline. He was quite capable, but we thought it would be to our advantage if we limited his responsibility by assuming the burden of play calling while he just played. We still had quarterback meetings three times a week so he would recognize the reasons for a game plan, but even though he appeared to understand, we called the plays. About midway through his junior year, we felt it was time to let him call his own plays, because a quarterback will usually execute a play of his own choosing with greater authority than one which is imposed on him. Prior to our first quarterback meeting that week, we informed him that he would direct the offense on Saturday, calling his own plays. Not to say that he paid more attention, because he was always a serious player, but following the meeting he asked if he could take film and a projector back to his room so he could study the game plan. Now here is a young man who never asked for the films until he knew *his name* would appear on the direction of the offense in a game and he suddenly wanted to be sure. Jeff Komlo became one of our finest quarterbacks and started fourteen games in the NFL following his graduation from Delaware.

You can't interact well with your players through a third person, you have to do it yourself. If you are trying to emulate your favorite coach, that third person will get in your way of commmunicating with a player. Be yourself! In reality it is impossible to be someone else anyway.

We are all guilty of repeating words or phases until they become trite and lose their meaning. Football coaches are especially guilty!

They'll grab what sounds like a great phrase and make a sign out of it. "It isn't the size of the fight but the dog in it" or something like that. We call them "box top" phrases and have become so sensitive to that kind of negative inspiration that one time we had a mixed metaphor spot on our bulletin board just for laughs. One especially memorable one was, "it isn't the fish in the barrel, but the number of rungs on the ladder." Use them for laughs, if you must, but avoid worn out cliches. They demean those movement provoking things that you want to say later.

"Setting goals" is another trite phrase. Everyone who talks about motivation says that establishing goals is a must for motivation. It's the fulfillment of these goals that reinforces effort and keeps a person going. It is better to encourage a young man to establish a plan for his life as well as for his participation in sports.

We all know that "setting personal goals" can be an effective motivational technique. A person setting a series of goals can see that his progress and his efforts are reinforced. We, however, talk to our players about developing a plan because the concept of "goal setting" is trite. Talk to them about creating their own plan, then urge them to go after it. Making a plan does two things; it outlines a series of short-range objectives and it forces a person to verbalize the things he really wants. Remember, if you can help a man get what he wants, he'll do virtually anything for you!

WIN ONE FOR THE GIPPER

Movies, stories, and television all depict, usually in an unflattering light, the pregame or half-time "pep talk." They have alerted the public in general and players, in particular, to look on football coaches as at least slightly demented. They create a suspicion of coaches and their actions. There is a plan, supported by physiological theory, to get your team mentally "ready" to play.

A player who is psychologically prepared to play is one who has completely focused his attention on the job at hand (the game), specifically his assignments and the part that he will play within the general plan of the team. In other words, concentration! He is able to wipe out thoughts of anything but the game. Nothing interferes with his preparation to play. This situation creates the physiological response for fight: adrenalin, constriction of the eyes, direction of the blood flow from internal organs to large muscle groups, a total physiological situation for action! Now, it becomes apparent that a player who is in this condition for long periods of time before a game is going to be a very tired player, so you must direct your teaching to create this response at just the right time. This is why people think that a coach can bring his team to a fevered emotional pitch just before the game with a brilliantly contrived pep talk, or as the story has it, "Win one for the Gipper!"

You will recall in our first orientation letter that the primary requirement of a succcessful team is that it plays with great intensity. This is the beginning of establishing a fundamental hardness that must be reached to build a successful team. You are asking for a consistant level of effort that will establish a hitting and running quality that will prevail during all of your practices. This is the beginning of establishing an emotional equilibrium for your team. Great bursts of emotionalism in play tend to tire the players. You want to create a high level of intensity as a general rule and not just for a single game.

You should, however, plan some spikes in emotion for particular games that require a superior effort. You can make a reference to a particuarly strong opponent or to games in which you will need a superior effort during preseason and at other times during the preparation for that opponent. The beginning of a "spiked performance" game week should be business-like but not emotional. Remember, it is tiring to be emotional. Let things build! Your players want to look good on game day. They want to win! Don't get in their way!

If you expect your team to be "ready" to play, remove distractions from your practices and locker rooms. While music may be appropriate in the locker room, equipment room, or training facilities early in the week, quiet the day before the game and especially during the last few hours before the game is much more effective. Give the players an uninterrupted opportunity to concentrate on their assignments. Some players don't like the pressure of silence, but I have found comfortable players don't play particularly well. Before the game, use the natural stimulants that surround the team. The sounds of game day are everywhere before the game—the band and crowd is exciting. Get your team off their feet and have a quiet period before you take the field. During last minute instructions and announcements to the starting offense, appeal for poise and speak reassuringly. But when talking to defensive players, raise your voice and appeal to their emotion, which they will need to play well. While offense is poised intensity, defense is played with great emotion. Just before they leave for the field, you can repeat the concern you planted during the preseason and made known through your preparation, to create some excitement by reminding them of their part before the game. This gives a rise to the pregame pep talk response. A good way to do this is to make a natural comment at the right time that will trigger a very personal reaction from each player.

Here is a review of the psychological principles for football coaches:

1. The ability to communicate with the players is the most important attribute a coach can have. Be honest and be yourself!

2. Two things motivate: Fear of failure and anticipation of reward.

3. View motivation from the players' standpoint—be subtle, no one wants to be manipulated.

4. Be sensitive to individual needs even though football is a team sport. The most successful motivating technique may be to help each player get what he wants!

5. Answer questions before they are asked. A well-informed team doesn't ask why.

6. Create an atmosphere of "ownership". The team belongs to the players, not the coaches.

7. Self-esteem begins with a sense of autonomy. Make the players responsible.

8. Successful pep talks are the result of certain circumstances and are not staged.

9. Save your team's emotional energy. Create stability.

10. Avoid the use of trite phrases.

11. Help your players develop a plan.

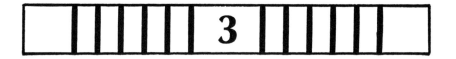

PHILOSOPHY AND DESIGN
OF THE DELAWARE WING-T

Football fads, fashions, and cycles have made offensive formation nicknames popular. Terms like *Wishbone* and *Pro and I Formation* have been used to describe attacks. While these terms are sometimes descriptive, they are often misleading, because few offensive systems use a single formation or style of moving the ball.

There are, however, four categories into which most offenses fall. They are: The Pro formations—two back-running formations with two wide receivers; the I Formation, which is sometimes a three-back running attack but more often two, and depends heavily on the tailback to carry the ball; the Wishbone or Full T, which are four-back attacks making a balance of running and passing difficult; and, finally, the single-back offense that has only the one set back and four receivers.

While there are strengths and weaknesses in every formation, we have avoided for the most part the pro formation because of its overdependence on the passing game; the I Formation because of its weakness outside and its inability to get the fourth receiver into a pattern; and the Wishbone for its lack of balance between running and passing.

MORE THAN A FORMATION

The Wing-T is more than a formation. It is a system of offense that is versatile and multiple in nature. It is best described as a four-back formation that originates as a running offense. However, the presence of the wing forces a defense to play at least three deep. In spite of its dependence on the running game, it is, paradoxically, initially dependent on the threat of a passing game. The passing, however, is action in nature with the quarterback keeping the ball with or away from the

19

flow of attack. It may be best described as sequence football. This should not imply that every play is run in order, but that the offense is run in series where several points are threatened as the ball is snapped. Its sequential aspect is shown not only from the series pattern of the backs but, just as significantly, from its blocking.

These sequential conflicts can be created in the following way:

(1) Multi-threats built within each backfield series, combining run and pass. Using the Belly series as an example, the systems can attack the defense off-tackle (Figure 3-1a), up the middle with a counter trap (Figure 3-1b), outside with an option (Figure 3-1c), or outside with a play-action pass (Figure 3-1d).

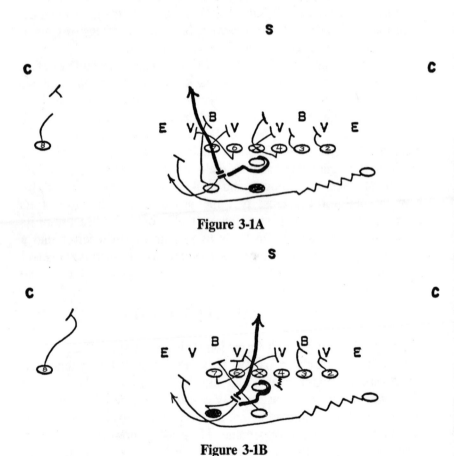

Figure 3-1A

Figure 3-1B

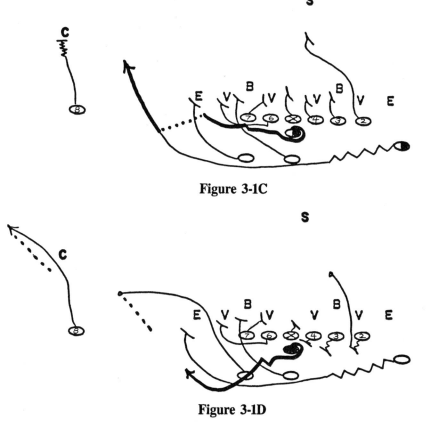

Figure 3-1C

Figure 3-1D

(2) Interrelating lineblocking schemes within each series and using similar blocking schemes with different backfield series. The basic Wing-T blocking scheme, which has the attack-side players block down, is designed to enable the system to run outside (Figure 3-2a), off-tackle (Figure 3-2b), or up the middle (Figure 3-2c). It is interesting that lineblocking schemes can create defensive conflicts independent of the backfield action. Figures 3-2a and 3-2c have the fullback going up the middle whereas Figure 3-2b has the fullback going off-tackle.

(3) Utilizing the misdirection theme to its fullest from similar backfield action. Because the Wing-T is a three-back offense, it can develop misdirection to its fullest.

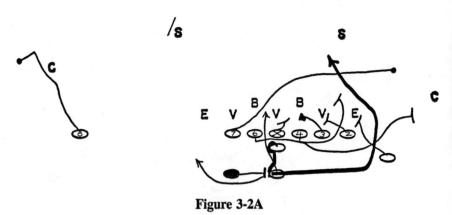

Figure 3-2A

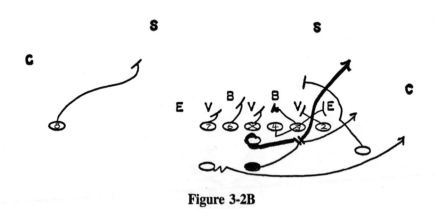

Figure 3-2B

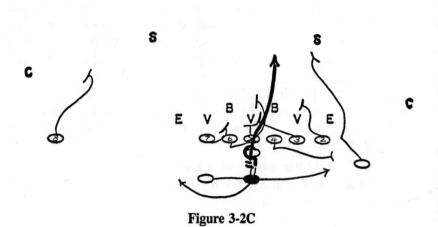

Figure 3-2C

    a) Motion: The system can develop misdirection first by
attacking the defense away from motion. This can be done by
having the quarterback keep the ball outside after faking to the
motion back (Figure 3-3a), by having the left halfback run off-
tackle in the direction opposite the motion (Figure 3-3b), or by
giving the ball to the motion back and having him run up the
middle (Figure 3-3c).

    b) To Wing: The system can also provide misdirection by
starting the backfield flow toward the wingback and having the
quarterback keep the ball outside after faking to the dive back
(Figure 3-4a). Using the same backfield action the system can
attack off-tackle away from flow by executing a halfback to
halfback reverse (Figure 3-4b).

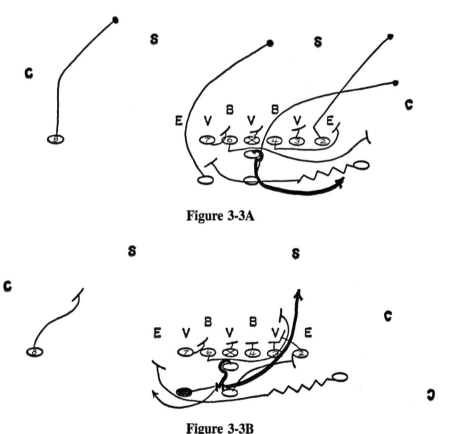

Figure 3-3A

Figure 3-3B

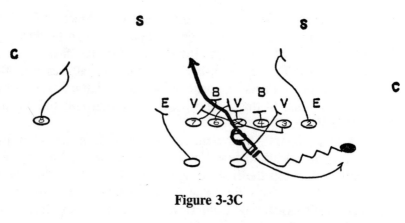

Figure 3-3C

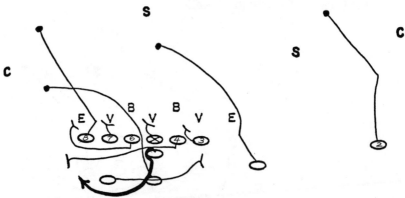

Figure 3-4A

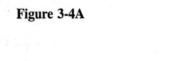

Figure 3-4B

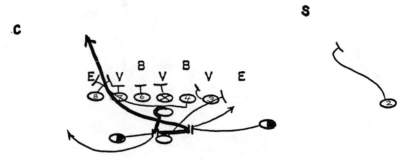

These series are designed to place as many conflicts on the defense as possible and are directed at men who have dual defensive assignments. The blocking style is designed so that as a defensive man reacts to the blocking in his area to stop a particular threat, he will be placing himself in jeopardy for a companion play. The defensive left tackle in Figure 3-5 faces such a conflict. If he reacts down with the tackle, he becomes vulnerable to the tight end block. Notice that the wing is threatening the end who is similarly affected. It is of interest to see that two distinct series are used for this example, and they both demonstrate inclination for the defensive linemen to watch backfield action. This, of course, is what the offense is attempting to do.

The philosophy of attack is based on the idea of taking advantage of the adjustments a defense must make to compensate for the wing's flanking angle. The seven-man front, for example, must do something

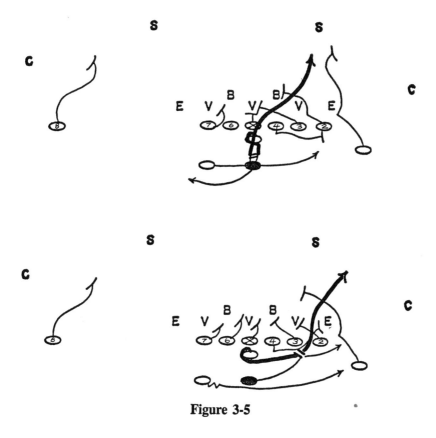

Figure 3-5

with their secondary, which will in turn weaken one flank or make them vulnerable to the pass. Against the eight-man front, the wing tends to widen the front creating a weakness off-tackle or up the middle. The three-deep secondary also feels the need to play men-pass defense in order to get adequate support at the flank to the wing. This increases the vulnerability of the defense to a weak side running and passing threat with the use of quick motion.

The offense includes the option from the fullback slant or belly series, but is not a triple option. It is advantageous to use several ways of attacking the flank because of the pressure this places on the end and, as a result, the triple would consume too much practice time. The quarterback will, however, threaten the flank at different depths. Threatening the flank adds a dimension to the defense of the front and provides an aspect of misdirection that is nonexistent in some systems. The quarterback will threaten the flank at a depth of six yards from the line of scrimmage when running the Waggle, or keep pass and tight to the line when running an option.

BASIC PRINCIPLES

The Wing-T has enjoyed the compliment of emulation and has proved successful at every level of football. Its inherent flexibility has allowed it to adjust successfully to defensive trends for over two decades and yet the following basic principles have remained:

1. The Wing-T is designed for consistency and strength and is ball control oriented.

2. The formations are characterized by a wing so that there is the threat of at least three deep receivers.

3. The quarterback threatens the flank either with action or away from it on every play providing either an additional threat to the attack flank or misdirection threatening the flank away from flow.

4. All three backs are close enough to the formation so that they can be used as blockers, ball carriers, or for deception.

5. The offense is designed in complete backfield series, each of which presents multiple threats to the defense on each play.

6. It has a balance of passing, which is predominantly play-action in nature.

7. The spread of receivers is accomplished by ends and is made to accommodate the running game as well as a mechanism to enhance the passing game.

GROUND ORIENTED

The objective of offense in football is, of course, to move the ball and score; but every coach is confronted with the question, "How can this be done most efficiently?" The conception of any football system must begin with deciding whether the attack will be primarily running or passing. Certainly, every offense must create a balance between running and passing, but because of limited practice time, the design must favor one phase.

The Delaware offense is primarily a running attack for the following reasons:

1. The core of any football team is hardness and as there is no separation of offense from defense, the style of offense affects the defense. The development of a gruelling consistent ground game builds a desire to dominate the opponent physically. How the ball is moved then shares importance with moving the ball itself.

2. During a football game, each team will get the ball between ten and fifteen times. The team that controls the ball by making first downs with the least risk of turning the ball over will decrease their opponent's opportunities to have the ball.

3. A consistent ground game increases the number of opportunities to enter the all important four-down area.

4. The running game is not as subject to severe weather problems as a passing game.

5. The running attack is not as dependent on the superior ability of one or two players as a primarily passing attack is.

BALANCE OF PASSING

In spite of the advantages of a sound running game, no offense can operate effectively today without a balance of passing. The defense often dictates what can be run effectively. Overaggressive secondary support and plugging linebackers can make it difficult to move the ball on the ground. Consequently, the passing game is designed to hit those areas that are covered by defenders whose immediate assignments must be to control the ground game. Play-action passes create defensive conflicts that make it difficult for these defenders to concentrate on either phase. In this way, the passing game complements the rushing game.

The offensive philosophy includes a great regard for the passing phase of football, which should be regarded not only as a scoring phase, but as a method of maintaining the ball. Passes that come from running action are most effective on early downs and enhance your chances of controlling the ball.

Basic Alignment

The Wing-T is a multiformation offense. The position of the backs should be constant, however, in order to maintain the balance and deception that is the basis of the entire system. The established positions for the backs are:

The Wingback: A wing is present in every formation for the following reasons:

a. It confronts the defensive secondary with an immediate threat of three deep receivers.

b. It widens the defensive front.

c. It presents an additional blocker at the line of scirmmage.

d. The motion of the wing balances the attack.

e. The motion of the wing creates misdirection.

The Halfback: Most of our formations will place at least one man in a dive position. This is important for the following reasons:

a. It enables the dive man to release quickly into a pass pattern as the fourth receiver.

b. It is an adequate position to block at the flank.

c. It provides a vertical blocking angle on linebackers and linemen.

The Fullback: The Fullback is in the middle of the formation for the following reasons:

a. It provides a dive threat to the middle of the defense.

b. It provides the offense with a balanced attack to either side of the formation, much the same as an I-formation tailback.

c. It enables the FB to flood either flank as a third receiver.

d. It solidifies the counter game by having the FB in a position to check.

Although the QB is under the center, as is the case with all modern offenses, his keeping the ball or faking away from the flow of attack presents the defense with an additional contain problem that minimizes pursuit and provides big play opportunities.

The Delaware Wing-T then, is a multiple formation, four-back running attack that depends heavily on play-action passing and misdirection, utilizing synchronized schemes both in the line-blocking and backfield action.

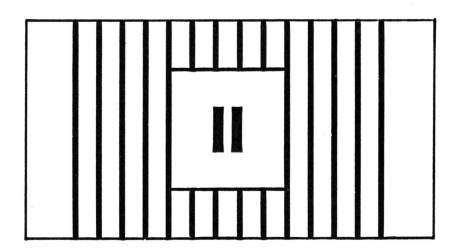

THE DEFENSES

A STUDY OF DEFENSES

Let us introduce the study of defenses by showing you how we number defensive men and recognize their defensive assignment probabilities. This system not only helps our quarterback read and recognize defenses, but it also provides a communication tool that helps us during both practice and games.

Begin by counting the first defensive man from the center's attack side gap and count towards the flank. The third man (3) must be considered as the contain of that flank. The fourth man (4) must be considered as the force of that flank and may also be assigned to cover the flat. The fifth man (5) will cover the deep corner of play patterns while the sixth (6) man will be interpreted as pursuit. (Figure 4-1).

It should be recognized that these assignments may be changed, but initially when running the option, the first two men will be assigned the first threat, (3) will have the quarterback while (4) has the pitch. These assignments may be changed by a defensive stunt or by some type of flow by the defense as the flank is threatened, but it is an effective technique to begin the recognition of a defense.

We refer to linebackers and men in the secondary as "mirror men" who will mirror the position of action or the ball. They will drop when the quarterback drops and roll when the ball threatens the flank. This of course forces them to declare their responsibility of contain, pitch, and flat.

There are three categories of defenses: three deep with an eight-men front; four deep with a seven-man front; and an unbalanced defense formed by the rotation of a four-deep defense or by moving a three-deep alignment over. Within each category, the spacing may be "odd", with a defensive man on the center, "even" with defensive men on your guards, or gapped with defensive men playing seam. The secondary coverage in these three categories may be played three deep "zone", four deep zone, or man, or in any combination of these three secondaries. The strength of these defenses may be studied by an

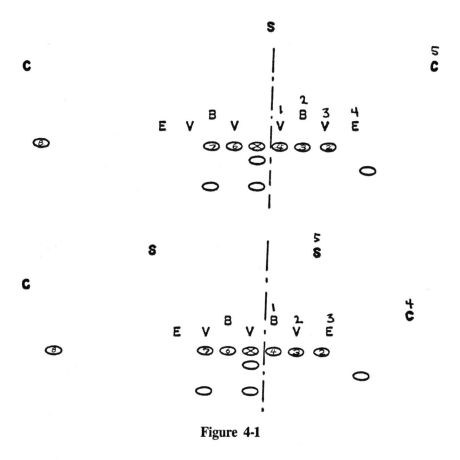

Figure 4-1

analogy of the first two, three-deep and four-deep. The third may fit into either category.

A three-deep defense will generally have two men on the line of scrimmage outside the offensive tackle (Figure 4-2), while the four-deep defense will generally only have one man on the line outside of your offensive tackle (Figure 4-3). You will recognize that your tight end seldom has a man playing on him against a four-deep defense and almost always has one on him from a three-deep defense.

While there are unlimited possibilities of alignments internally, there is a general characteristic to each type of defense. Three-deep defenses have four defensive men over five offensive men from tackle to tackle (Figure 4-4). Four-deep defenses have five men aligned over the same area, but the defense may be reduced so that six men will play

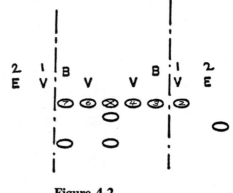

Figure 4-2

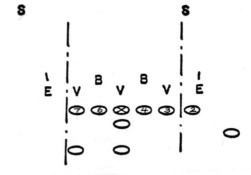

Figure 4-3

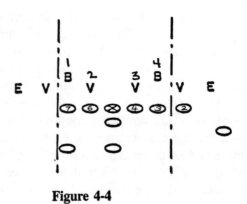

Figure 4-4

over your internal five (Figure 4-5). The recognition and attack of this specific problem will be discussed later.

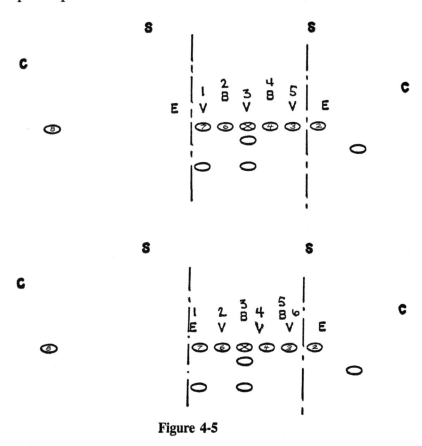

Figure 4-5

ADJUSTMENTS OF THE FOUR-DEEP DEFENSE

The four-deep secondary should be regarded as divided into two pairs of two, assigned to the coverage and support of the flank on their side. One of the pair will support aggressively or cover the flat while the other stays deep (Figure 4-6). The side away from action may tend to flow, forming a three-deep picture, or hang as in two-deep. The support of a flank may come from the corner back outside or from the safety inside forming inverted support. Some four-deep teams may support with both safety and corner back, bringing the offside safety all the way across the formation for deep half coverage.

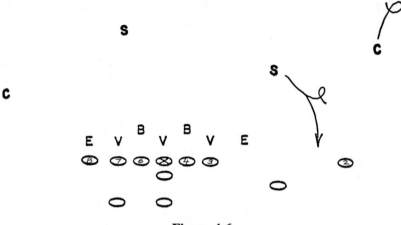

Figure 4-6

The four-deep defense is often played with two safeties playing deep half and the corner backs playing force or flat. This two-deep secondary may not react to offensive flow at all (Figure 4-7).

The ability to flow, however, makes the four-deep defense a most versatile secondary, giving you several adjustments from it.

The coverage of the flat is not a great problem for the four-deep defense, but it is most always covered from the front by one of the two defenders on that side. When the safety inverts and covers it, we refer to this action as "switch". This easily forms a three-deep secondary (Figure 4-8). When the halfback covers it, we call this adjustment "split" coverage. This action is also referred to as roll up and becomes a two-deep secondary (Figure 4-9).

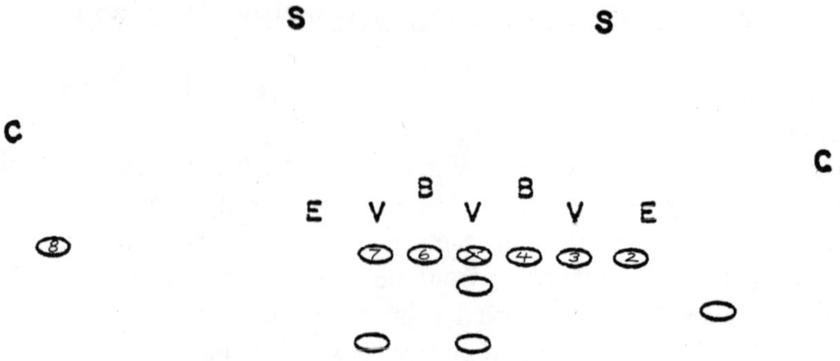

Figure 4-7

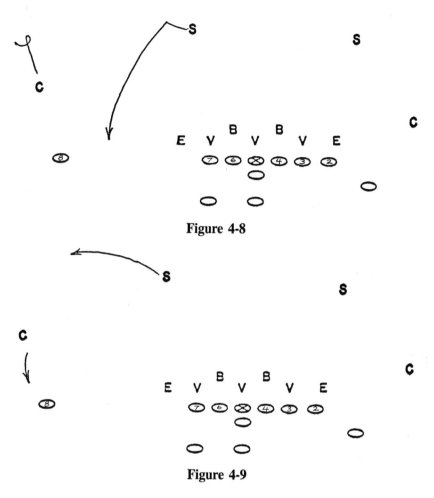

Figure 4-8

Figure 4-9

The third category is "man" coverage. Each of the pair on either side will pick up the end and the first back out of the formation on their side, while a backer picks up the second man out (Figure 4-10).

There are several combinations possible. Half may be played as "zone" with a free safety, "zone" with two-deep type side, or man while the other half is played another way.

ADJUSTMENTS OF THE THREE-DEEP DEFENSE

The men in the three-deep secondary are pass coverage oriented and generally depend on the front eight to control the running game. The

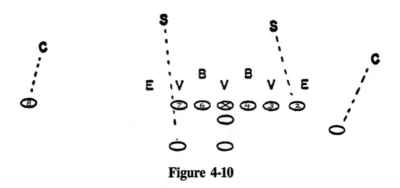

Figure 4-10

three-deep secondary is limited in the adjustments it is capable of making but may flow with action to the flank of a tight side, releasing the halfback to support or cover the flat. This technique will be referred to as an "up," "level off," or "roll up" and leaves the secondary in two-deep. Number 4 must contain the quarterback while 5 revolves to the flat. Now the safety (6) comes to strong half (Figure 4-11). If a threat is made to a flank with a spread receiver, the "up" technique becomes risky as the spread receiver is too wide for the safety man to cover deep (Figure 4-12).

When running an action pass to a spread receiver you will force the defense to cover the flat with a lineman. This places a great stress on the corner, because one lineman must react to the running threat and one must control the quarterback while a third must cover the flat.

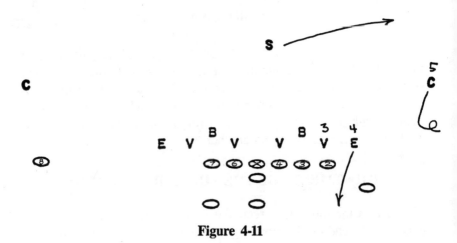

Figure 4-11

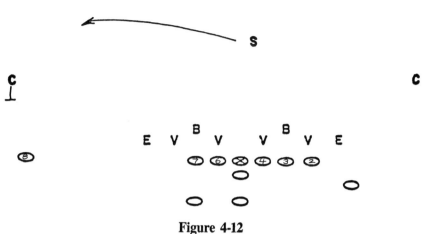

Figure 4-12

The flats of a three-deep defense are generally covered from underneath with a linebacker unless some adjustment is made to cover them with a back. The defense is as aware of this problem as you are and will take some risk with their deep coverage to firm up the defense of the flank to a spread receiver. Some will "up," exposing themselves to deep sideline and flag problems, while still others will invert the single safety for man coverage, exposing the post cut. (Figure 4-13).

If you show an unbalanced line to a three-deep defense, the defense must move its spacing to adjust to your strength. This places the defensive front in a new alignment, and may force an unfamiliar reaction. (Figure 4-14).

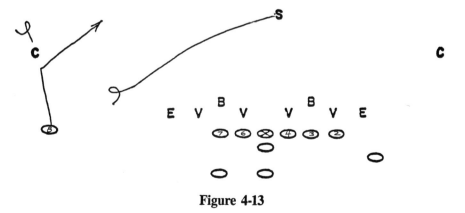

Figure 4-13

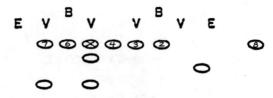

Figure 4-14

ATTACKING THE DEFENSE

The following suggestions for attack are made not to restrict your thinking to a narrow program of personal concepts, but rather in an attempt to demonstrate the way we would study a defense and develop a game plan. Just remember, any play that moves the ball is a good one and the unexpected is still the best call.

We have already demonstrated that formations create angles and certainly our basic Wing-T formation is no exception. While the wing is a spread of strength and not a change of strength it still forces some kind of adjustment from every defense. Strangely, eleven defensive men can't be divided equally and one flank or the other will create a flanking angle.

When attacking any defense, inspect the adjustment to four basic flanks: tight end and wing, spread end and slot back, spread end and diveman, and tight end and diveman. These four flanks are available from your 100-900 and spread 100-900 formations. Red and Blue (double wing) are combinations of these two basic formations.

When selecting a flank, look first at your strong flank, then answer the questions: Has the defense adjusted to strength? For example: Are they ready to meet strength with strength?!

How close is 4 to the flank? Has 3 adjusted to your wing, and how committed is he to sealing? Who will contain the flank, with action, without action? (Figure 5-1).

When planning your attack, create as many conflicts as possible. Recognize men who have dual responsibilities. Your offense is designed to confront these men with an either/or choice. If they react to stop one play, they will place themselves in jeopardy for a companion play. Direct the flow of your attack toward the flank with the most advantageous angle to place pressure on that flank.

Attempt to plan an attack with only a handful of plays, which we refer to as "primary." The others come from the establishment of these select plays.

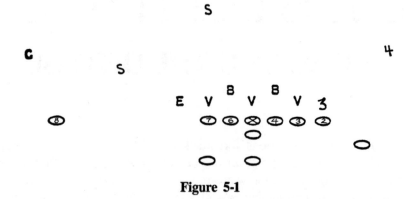

Figure 5-1

In spite of the fact that we number the points of attack over offensive linemen there are really only three points of attack on either side of the center: (1) outside, (2) off tackle, and (3) up the middle. The attack of each area should be related to the adjacent area (Figure 5-2).

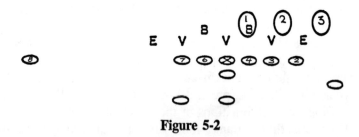

Figure 5-2

ATTACKING THE FLANK OF THE FOUR DEEP

After categorizing the defense as four deep, check its alignment and adjustment to your flanks. Look at their adjustment to your wing first.

Recognize that your wing outflanks 3. This should force 4 to rotate to the line or be conscious of support. The spread end should have a crack-back angle on their inverted safety or force the corner to support wide. The off flank of a formation may well be as important as the primary flank and either flank may indicate a weakness.

Remember, your offense is a flow offense that threatens several points of attack with each action. When selecting a flank you should include the package of plays that originate from the particular flow. These plays should especially include your play-action passes.

Consider running to the tight end and wing first. Have they met strength or have they dropped off rotating to the spread end or wide side? Defensive hash mark consideration is often more important than your formation. If 4 to the wing flank is off the line of scrimmage, you have 3 outflanked. Block down on him with your wing. You have both the 20s and 30s available. (Figure 5-3). If 3 is soft, blow him out with the power of the 30s. If he is reading your tight end, encourage him to seal down as your tight end blocks down. This will make him vulnerable to your wing. They should not be able to stop this attack until 4 comes to the line of scrimmage or the fifth man supports, i.e. both corner and safety.

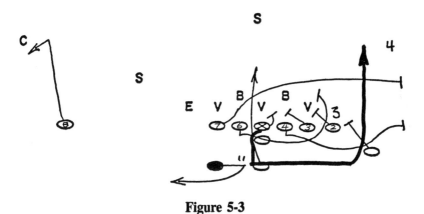

Figure 5-3

If you find that the cornerback (4) and the safety (5) are interested in "man" coverage and both support quickly when your wing and tight end block down, run at that flank with a release, i.e., 121 Release or 182 Down with the wing releasing. "Man" defenses have trouble supporting the option when a receiver releases deep at that flank.

Recognize the pressure you have placed on their end. He is outflanked by your wing, yet he must be ready to seal the tight end shoulder and still control the quarterback if he keeps the ball on the option. For example, 182 Down Option (Figure 5-4).

Naturally, you can't answer all of the questions about their defense with one cursory look. Acquire the ability to collect information with each play. Certainly, when faking the bootleg, the quarterback can read the offside defense in general, and the free safety specifically. Remember, he could very well become the sixth man at

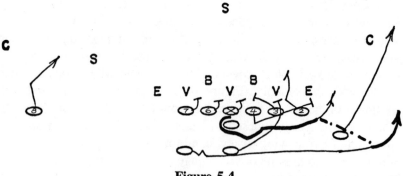

Figure 5-4

the flank either by rotating or flowing. You should force the defense to stop your wing attack. Force them to rotate! This attack should force their free safety to the middle of the formation. The fourth man to the weak side now assumes the responsibility of the fifth and is isolated on our spread end. Now use your waggle away form the wing. Use individual cuts to the spread end or dump the ball to the FB. We will discuss the total waggle "read" and techniques later.

When a good sound adjustment is made to your wing, don't run at it (Figure 5-5). As Woody Hayes said, "Don't attack walled cities." Now look at the flank away from the wing and see how this adjustment to your wing has affected their defense of your flank away from your wing. A rotation to your wing may make the spread end flank away from the wing particularly vulnerable. The spread end is isolated and we have already suggested throwing to him from waggle action.

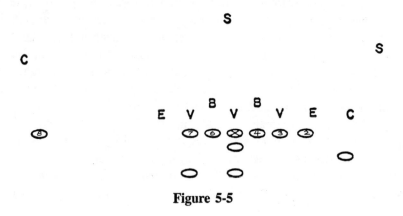

Figure 5-5

Inspect this flank. Locate 3's position. Locate 4 and determine his support angle (Figure 5-6). Continue to collect information. You will begin this attack with motion. Now determine the speed and extent of secondary flow to your weak flank and the support of that flank. Is it rolled (corner supported) or inverted (safety supported)? How fast and from what angle will 4 support? The answers to these questions build a passing attack later, and rapid flow suggests waggle and a "Z" attack (misdirection motion) back to the tight end flank.

Begin the attack of this flank with motion. When running to a spread end flank, consider the option attack first. You have both the belly and the trap options. Recognize 3's position and action. He has more freedom when playing to a spread end. If 3 crosses the line and is quarterback conscious, consider blocking him with your halfback and "loading" the option (Figure 5-7). This may provide an exceptional

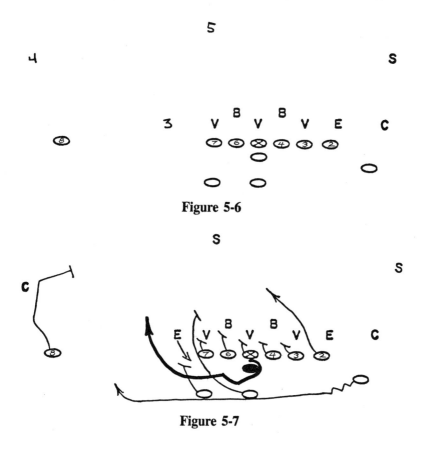

Figure 5-6

Figure 5-7

running opportunity for your quarterback. If the defensive front is reduced (i.e. moved toward your tight end) run your motion buck sweep there. The belly keep pass and trap option pass should be considered a phase of this attack.

By now, you should be able to determine 4's support angle. If he is the cornerback, releasing your end outside of him makes his support difficult. If the free safety inverts, crack back on him with the spread end. Inverted support however suggests option pass or belly keep pass post.

If you are getting a full secondary flow with this motion to your weak side, the waggle with motion to the tight end may be exceptional. If the flow is good enough to stop your attack of this flank with motion, consider running at it with two back plays i.e. 90 opt, or 80 No Mo pitch (Figure 5-8).

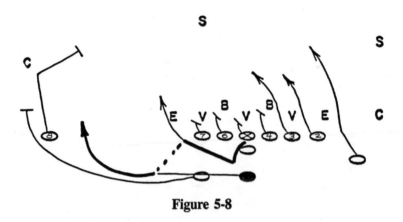

Figure 5-8

ATTACKING OFF TACKLE OF THE FOUR-DEEP

Your attack off tackle against the four deep was discussed somewhat in the flank attack and you must recognize they complement each other. Recognize that 3 must seal and contain to a tight end side and contain to a spread end side. Your end will seldom be covered by a defensive man and generally has a flanking position on 2. Use belly action to determine 3's assignment. If he is not concerned with the fullback, belly "down" will be an excellent play. (Figure 5-9). If he does close with the fullback, keep the ball with down option. Check his reaction to the inside release of your end and run waggle or "Z" sweep

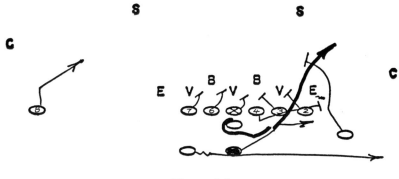

Figure 5-9

accordingly. The "Z" 82 Down is antagonistic to the containment of the waggle.

If 3 becomes conscious of your wing's block on him and stunts or works outside, kick him out with 30 power or 2 gut (Figure 5-10). The inside handoff to the halfback of the gut gives you a quick hitter here.

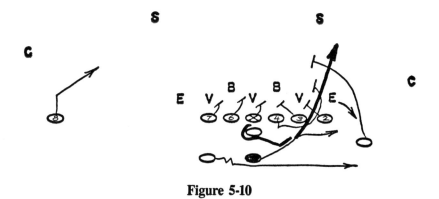

Figure 5-10

ATTACKING THE MIDDLE OF A FOUR-DEEP DEFENSE

The seven-man front of a four-deep defense that is played without reduction will place 5 men over your internal 5 and your ends are seldom covered. However, the defense has 6 seams to control even though they have 5 men over 5. Someone has a dual responsibility and initially you must consider the nose man in this capacity. In addition, the backers who also have dual jobs make the middle soft when they're concerned about pursuit outside.

Your attack up the middle is determined by defensive reaction and falls into four categories: (1) direct dive, (2) wind back, (3) trap (direct or counter), and (4) combination.

Begin this attack with "on" blocking to your fullback from the 20s, and X block from the belly. The fullback reads the action of the nose man on both plays. The belly looks like sweep for the first few steps and the backers tend to flow. The odd block off the back side becomes particularly effective when backers and nose chase (Figure 5-11).

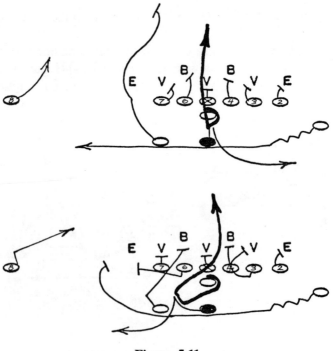

Figure 5-11

Now determine their tackle's reaction to your down blocking. If their tackle is not conscious of your tackle blocking down, run the counters at 4 and 6. If he goes down with your tackle use 23 blocking. That controls the defensive tackle and the guard gut blocks the linebacker (Figure 5-12). They may also be run with your dive man depending on their backer's reaction.

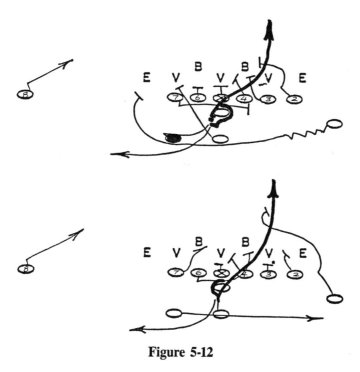

Figure 5-12

ATTACKING THE FLANK OF A THREE-DEEP DEFENSE

Inspect their adjustments to your flanks. Locate 3 and 4 at each flank. Three will probably be on the inside shoulder of your tight end and just outside your tackle at the flexed flank. Four will probably be near the line of scrimmage. If it is a true eight-man front, it will be a balanced defense. Look at the first procedure of attacking three-deep, i.e. adjust the positions of your ends. Adjust your formation to pressure 3 and 4. Increase the flex of your tight end to six feet, and reduce the distance of your spread end to from four to six yards. The tight end's flex will force 3 to commit his area of responsibility and the reduction of the spread receiver will place 4 in jeopardy (Figure 5-13). If 3 plays inside your tight end, begin your attack exactly as you did against four deep. Run to that flank with the 20s and 80 Down Option. When running the option, consider the aspect of keeping the ball rather than pitching, as 4 is in good position to accept the pitch responsibility (Figure 5-14). However, 3 has the incredibly difficult job of controlling both the fullback off the corner and the quarterback, keeping the ball. In all probability your fullback game will be great. If 3 moves out with your

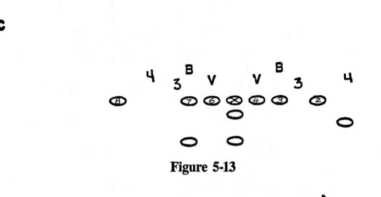

Figure 5-13

Figure 5-14

tight end, forget the flank and drive the ball with your fullback inside of 3.

The flank away from the wing may be as vulnerable as that to the wing. If 4 is dropped off to the split, the end has a flanking position on him. In all probability, 3 will play your tackle's shoulder, giving your halfback a shot at him. Use the same attack away from the wing, but include the buck sweep. You have angles on everyone (Figure 5-15).

Your action passing game is an important aspect of your flank attack against a three-deep defense. There are two types of action passes at the flank: (1) keep passes, when you keep the ball to the flank with play action and (2) waggle passes, when you threaten the flank away from the action. Because the three-deep coverage of the flat is from underneath to a split end, keep passes tend to force that coverage to contain the ball.

The split of the end should force either 2 or 4 to cover the flat; a wide release by the end would make the level-off difficult. Throwing into the flat should be regarded as part of your running attack. Release

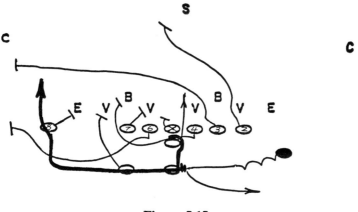

Figure 5-15

a man into the flat and run the split end deep (Figure 5-16). If they level off, the end will sideline deep (Figure 5-17).

Run the same type of play to the wing with the wing releasing wide and deep. If the wing releases properly, the secondary will not be able to "up" and you will have forced the same problem to the wing as to the flexed end (Figure 5-18).

Attacking Off Tackle of Three Deep

When your halfbacks carry the ball, the attack is delayed at both the flank and inside. When the halfbacks carry inside all of the

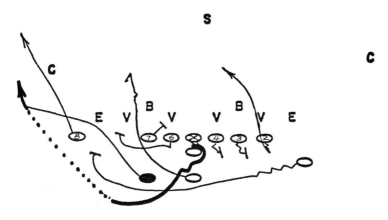

Figure 5-16

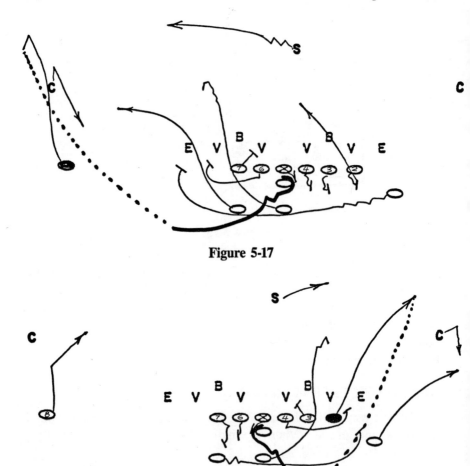

Figure 5-17

Figure 5-18

blocking is double team trap. This, of course, is a very valuable aspect of your offense, but, like the pitcher's change of speed in baseball, you need a quick hitting phase of attack also. Your fullback attack supplies a variation of hitting speeds to your offense, and is used with predominantly one on one blocking.

You can hit off tackle with quick fullback shots at two and eight with predetermined blocking (Figure 5-19), or delayed at three or seven where the fullback reads daylight. That is, use an opening that is created by the defense itself as it overpursues (Figure 5-20). Remember, against any defense there are only three places to run. Off

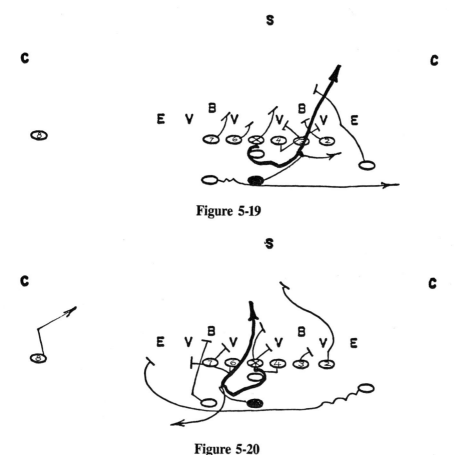

Figure 5-19

Figure 5-20

tackle should attract your attention first when attacking a balanced eight-man front.

Your attack off tackle will complement your success outside and take advantage of the reaction and adjustments that have been made. Remember the key to offensive success is to force a defensive adjustment. Determine 3's play. He is your key in determining when you run outside or when you run inside. Use the action toward 3 that has been successful outside. If 121, for example, has been successful, and they react to it, then 122 Gut may be good (Figure 5-21). If 3 is conscious of your tight end's release, consider "gut release". Using the fullback quickly with down blocking should be difficult for them to stop, and if 3 becomes a factor in stopping this, use Down Option.

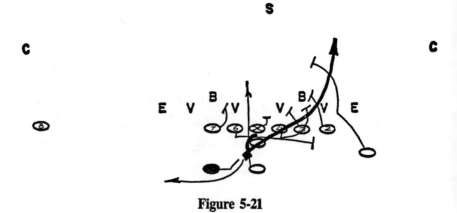

Figure 5-21

Recognize their problem of covering the action flat with 4, which forces 3 to contain leaving only 1 and 2 to stop the fullback, i.e., counter at two or right (Figure 5-22).

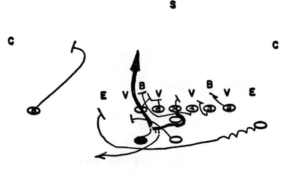

Figure 5-22

Attacking the Middle of the Three Deep

Your attack up the middle is determined by the defense's reaction to your action outside and off tackle, and falls in three categories: (1) direct dive, (2) counter, or (3) wind back.

Recognize that there are only four men from the outside shoulder of one tackle to the outside shoulder of the other, i.e., four defensive men over five defensive men. There is a natural hole. Your problem is to find it. The "wide tackle six" shows you the opening, over the center. The split six is a flowing internal defense. One linebacker will flow to the attack side while the other covers the middle. The wide tackle suggests guard trap while the "split six" suggests a combination of belly off the corner and counter up the middle. The wind-back belly is in the counter category. If the backers chase the guards on the twenty sweeps, use the "gut" up the middle against the "split six" (Figure 5-23).

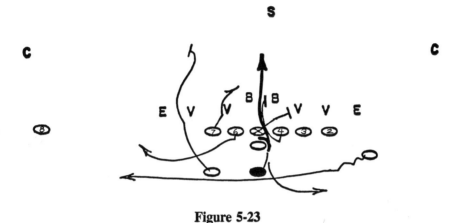

Figure 5-23

The Passing Game

Throwing must be a share of your total offensive concept. It should not be regarded as an offense within itself but a well-integrated aspect of your attack. It is not only a method of moving the ball but a technique for controlling defensive men.

The old adage of "throwing the ball where they ain't" may still be a good one, but it may help if you realize that it is difficult for a defender to cover a man in a pass pattern from a head-on-head position. When this happens, the receiver can break either way and gain a step. Most defenders will shade one way. Know where that defender is—it'll save you many headaches.

The defense will always have a perimeter. You can attack it with a "vertical stretch" (Figure 5-24) by running conflicting deep routes or with a "horizontal stretch" (Figure 5-25) by running wide and into the flat. You should remember that width is often more difficult to cover than depth.

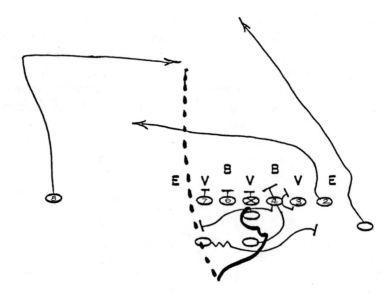

Figure 5-24

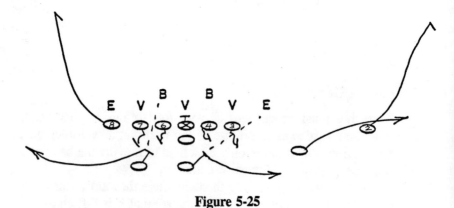

Figure 5-25

All zone defenses have mirror people (linebackers in underneath positions): men who will mirror the ball's action creating openings in front of the deep perimeter and behind them or in front of them, depending on your quarterback's movement with the ball, i.e., play action or drop back.

There are four techniques for creating an opening for a receiver: (1) having a wide out beat a defender with exceptional speed (this, of course, may be difficult) breaking outside of the perimeter; (2) moving through a seam between two or more defenders; (3) employing two receivers in an area creating an either/or situation; and (4) running away from coverage. Any and all of these techniques may use backfield action to assist in creating that situation.

Your passing attack can be placed in four categories: (1) action passes toward the flow, (2) action passes away from the flow, (3) drop back, and (4) sprint out. Each has its place and your success may rest in the selection of that place.

You should recognize by now that the role your passing attack will play is so interdependent with your running game that it is difficult to separate it, but when you elect to throw there are some principles that will guide your selection. First, take a look at the defensive responsibilities. The defense must assign someone to cover your spread end on both "out" and "in" cuts in addition to covering the deep threats of post, fly, and flag. The deep threat should create a cushion for short cuts. These will be covered by defensive backs. Next they must have someone to cover the flat, hooks, and curl—in most zones these will be covered by linebackers—(mirror men).

When preparing to pass, recognize the defensive alignment and answer the questions: What balance to your strength is made with their secondary? Is it three deep or four deep? Who will contain you and under what circumstances? What are the dual responsibilities of the linebackers and backs?

Passing Against Four Deep

When you are ready to throw, you should know how the secondary will react to the movement of your backfield action. You will recall that a four-deep secondary should be regarded as two pairs of two, and one back at the attack flank will be assigned to cover the flat and force the flank while the other will cover deep. The offside pair will either sit in zone or flow with your action. "Man" coverage will be recognized by tight inside out positions of the defensive backs and will probably be accompanied by pressure from linebackers.

The first use of our passing game should be to limit 5's support of the flank and force his concern with the problem of the corner coverage, i.e., out, in, and fly conflict. The deep threat should create a cushion when your spread receiver breaks outside of the defensive perimeter. You may throw to the wide out from several series. The situation and flow of the defense will assist you in that selection. Force 4 to become concerned about his support and throw into the flat.

Draw a line through the middle of your formation to determine whether or not they are meeting strength with strength (Figure 5-26). Remember eleven can't be divided by two evenly unless there is a man straddling or near the line. Unless the secondary is "man" or zone 200, the free safety will move toward your strength. Your wing gives you an immediate flat threat and should force some adjustment there. Remember, the release of two receivers at a flank creates several problems and will encourage one man (strong safety) on the side of strength to concentrate on short coverage areas. The wing release will

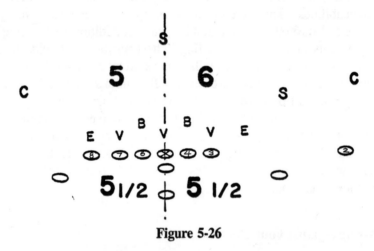

Figure 5-26

control underneath coverage or give you an alternate receiver. This will force the free safety to compensate for the strong seam problem and create what is tantamount to rotation (Figure 5-27).

If the defensive front is 55, only the free safety changes the balance. If the front is 40, (3 linebackers) the middle backer's drop indicates a change in strength. If the free safety is near the middle, look for a flank at which you have them outnumbered (Figure 5-28). Recognize that the position of your dive back makes a quick release to the weak flat possible. Look for seam openings against zone. Work on the weak side release away from the "spread" with tight end hook, dive man flare, or delayed release (Figure 5-29). You're working on a "horizontal stretch" of the defense. The conflict of coverage is from sideline to sideline.

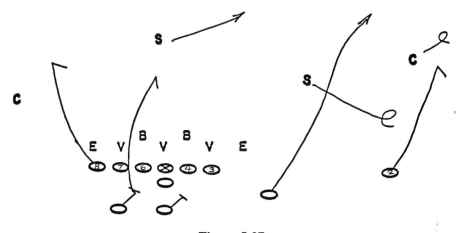

Figure 5-27

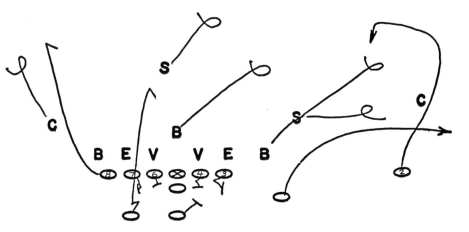

Figure 5-28

When you use the 50s, you will get quick drop reaction from the backer. Work in front of them with delays or screens! Be very conscious of the requirement of each down. The defense will be very conscious of the situation.

If the coverage is four-deep "man," all of your receivers will shorten their patterns and run away from coverage at right angles. Look for pressure. Get rid of the ball. Screens become particularly effective against "man" (Figure 5-30).

If the secondary rolls up to your spread receiver, or is in 200 instead of inverting, your "out" cut automatically becomes a "weave."

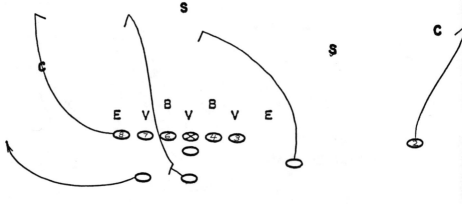

Figure 5-29

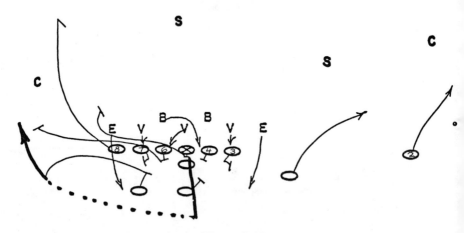

Figure 5-30

The wing or dive man will run flare, seam, or flat. Read 4 and throw to the open man. They are running as a pair to create an opening. Two hundred is easily identified by safety men. A 200 secondary is generally a poor adjustment against your spread formation. Double wing may also be tough against 200. The principle you should use against 200 is weave, or a two-deep release to one flank (Figure 5-31). You are now using what we will refer to as a "vertical stretch." Give the defense the conflict of covering more receivers deep than they are able to cover in addition to forcing 4 to cover, weave, or flat (Figure 5-32).

Your greatest chance of early-down passing success rests with your action passes. For example, the trap option pass toward a flank

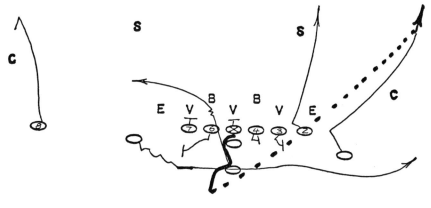

Figure 5-31

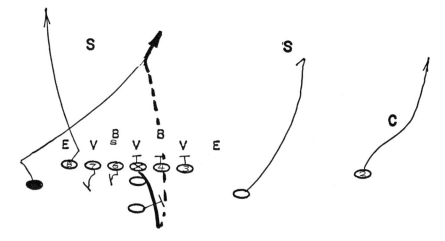

Figure 5-32

that you have already run a successful trap optic n against may be open. Once you have hit the end, the halfback or wing may be open (Figure 5-33). The waggle is an offense within itself against a four-deep defense. Make certain you know if the free safety will flow with your backfield action. This will direct your attention to the flank toward which you should throw (Figure 5-34).

Passing Against Three Deep

You will recall that the three-deep defense shows 4 at each flank on the line of scrimmage, and generally the free safety will play deep in the middle. This defense, while having its own merits, does not have

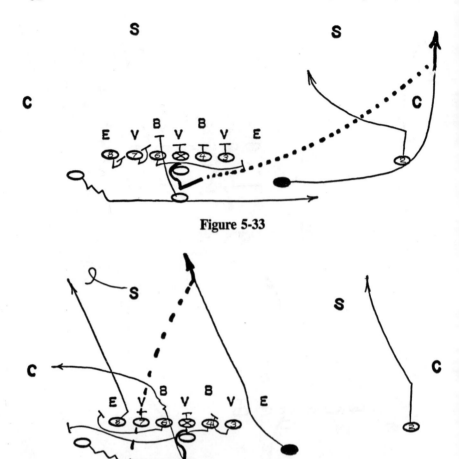

Figure 5-33

Figure 5-34

a great many adjustments and is somewhat static. The free safety may roll with action, freeing 5 to relinquish his deep responsibility to cover the flat while 4 contains the flank. This is however a defensive risk at best, which leaves the seam open for a period, while isolating the offside halfback (Figure 5-35).

We'll take three formation approaches to throwing against a three-deep defense: (1) reduce the flex of the wide out ("split", "slot") to pressure 4, making it difficult for him to decide to contain or cover the flat while being in jeopardy of being knocked down by the spread end; (2) extend the flex of the receiver while widening your wing to a flanker, leaving the free safety in the middle with nothing to do or; (3)

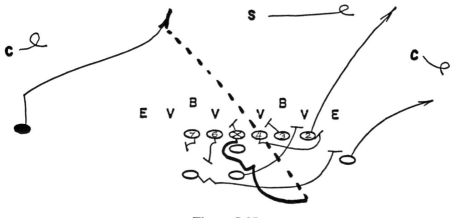

Figure 5-35

run from double wing threatening four-deep receivers while they have only three to cover. You could also use a combination of these three attacks (Figure 5-36).

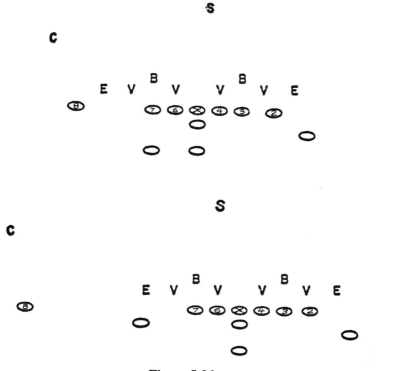

Figure 5-36

S

C   C

E V B V   V B V E

⑧   ⑦ ⑥ ⊗ ④ ③   ②
              ○
                        ○
        ○   ○

Figure 5-36 (continued)

Look at the reduction of the flex first. Action passes to the flank with a man in the flat and a receiver running through the seam with width places a great deal of pressure on 4. He's in the middle. The seams are always vulnerable when you are throwing against a zone. This action may take place toward either the strong flank (to a wing or slot) or to a spread receiver away from the strength (Figure 5-37). Now use your spread receiver all the way out. He is isolated on the defensive halfback without any real help except what 4 might give him by dropping. The free safety is out of it. Increase the problem using the pro wing. The safety man cannot do anything but cover a post. You have them outnumbered eleven to ten (Figure 5-38).

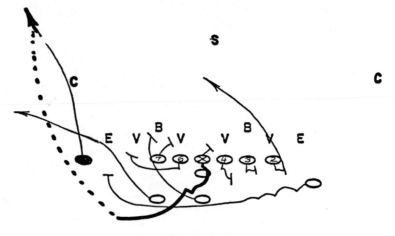

Figure 5-37

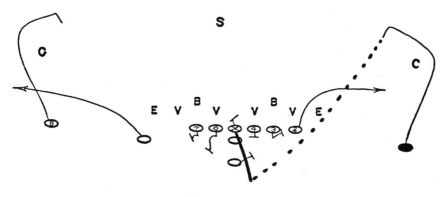

Figure 5-38

Consider a vertical stretch on their two halfbacks, throwing the ball wide or into the flat. Counter bootleg and keep passes should be your beginning because of the lack of defensive flexibility. Use the waggle for individual cuts or crossing, but the keep pass should take precedence. Occasionally let your four-deep receivers "jet" and find out which one is not covered (Figure 5-39).

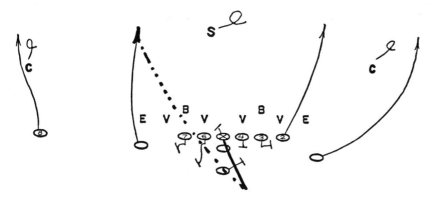

Figure 5-39

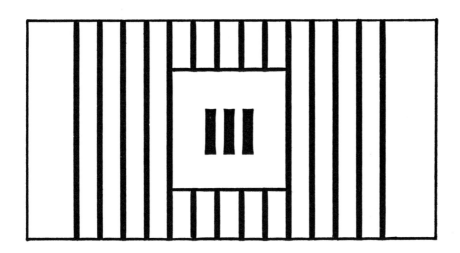

ELEMENTS OF THE OFFENSE

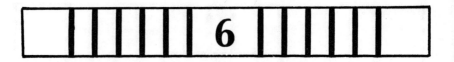
OFFENSIVE COMMUNICATION AND STRUCTURE

The advantage of offense over defense is knowing from what formation, how and where the play will attack and when the ball will be put in play. This, of course, requires a numbering system that clearly communicates an entire play simply and quickly.

The numbering system used in the Delaware Wing-T to communicate the information necessary for a play to be executed is combined into a three-digit numbering scheme. These three digits may be preceded by a term altering the formation and/or followed by a term modifying the play. The first digit indicates the formation, the second digit indicates the backfield series, and the third digit indicates the point of attack. This numbering scheme goes from right to left in ascending order beginning with one and ending with nine. One

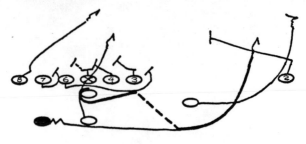

Figure 6-1

through four are therefore synonymous with right, while six through nine are synonymous with left. The following is our example of this three digit system.

PREFIX	FORMATION	SERIES	POINT OF ATTACK	SUFFIX
Spread	1	2	1	Trap Option

Alignment

There are several formations used in the Delaware Wing-T, but the alignment of personnel remains constant. The internal linemen, from tackle to tackle, line up as far off the ball as they legally can, i.e., their helmets in line with the base of the center's numbers. Their split is normally two feet, with the option to widen an additional foot when a defender is aligned head up. The spread end lines up opposite the wingback unless specifically told to modify this position. The normal width of the spread end is wide enough to force a four-deep defense to invert to the flexed side (approximately twelve to fifteen yards). The tight end splits three feet from the tackle if the tackle has a man on him and six feet if the tackle is uncovered. In the backfield, the wingback is two yards from the tight end, when he is split three feet, and two yards off the ball. The fullback's toes are four yards from the ball and the diveback is parallel with the fullback, thatching the outside foot of the tackle (Figure 6-2). The I formation stacks the dive man behind the fullback at a depth of five and one-half yards (Figure 6-3).

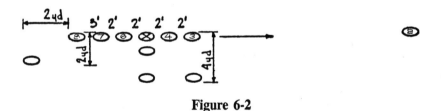

Figure 6-2

Figure 6-3

Formations

A wingback will line up on the right side when the first digit is one through four and on the left side when it is six through nine. Wing right is therefore 100 and Wing left is 900. 200-800 slides the fullback over to form split backs while 300-700 places both halfbacks to the designated side forming a strong set. Red (TE right) and Blue (TE left) place both halfbacks in a wing position (Figure 6-4)

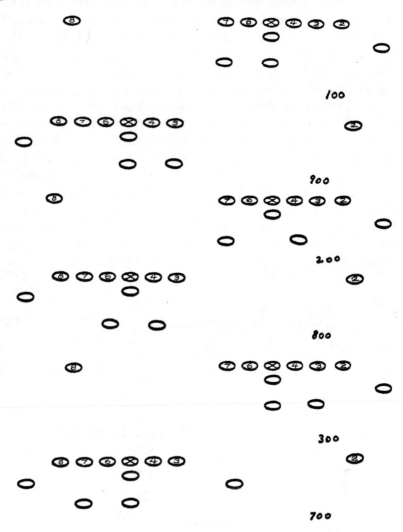

Figure 6-4

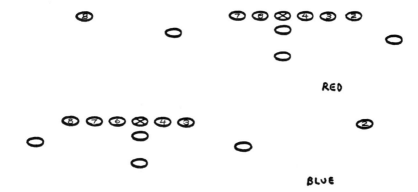

RED

BLUE

Figure 6-4 (continued)

The prefix can be either a word or a letter and modifies the formation by either adjusting an end or a back. The prefixes that adjust the ends are:

1. Split—Reduces the width of the spread end to four to six yards (Figure 6-5).
2. Spread—Places the spread end on the same side as the wingback (Figure 6-6).

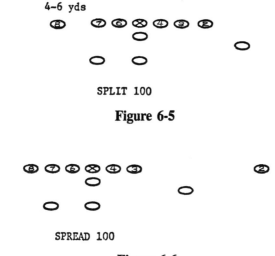

4-6 yds

SPLIT 100

Figure 6-5

SPREAD 100

Figure 6-6

3. Slot—Narrows the width of the spread end to the side of the wingback to six to eight yards (Figure 6-7).

4. Right (or Left)—Places both ends to the side designated (Figure 6-8).

5. Tight—Places both ends in the tight position (Figure 6-9).

6. Loose—Places both ends in the spread position (Figure 6-10).

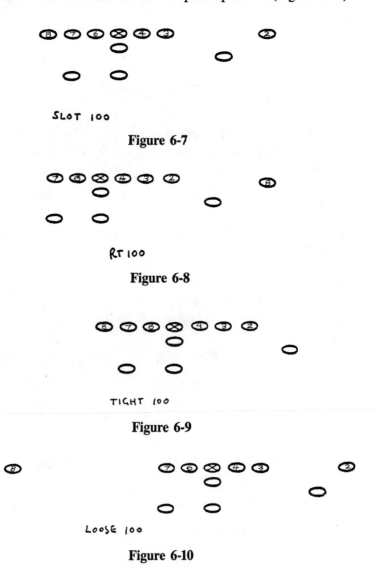

SLOT 100

Figure 6-7

RT 100

Figure 6-8

TIGHT 100

Figure 6-9

LOOSE 100

Figure 6-10

The prefixes that adjust the backs are:

1. I—Places the diveback stacked behind the fullback (Figure 6-11).
2. Pro—Moves the wingback out to a flanker position, twelve to fifteen yards from the tight end (Figure 6-12).
3. Twins—Moves the wingback out to a flanker position to the side of the spread end (Figure 6-13).
4. Trips—Places a wingback and a flanker to the side of the spread end (Figure 6-14).

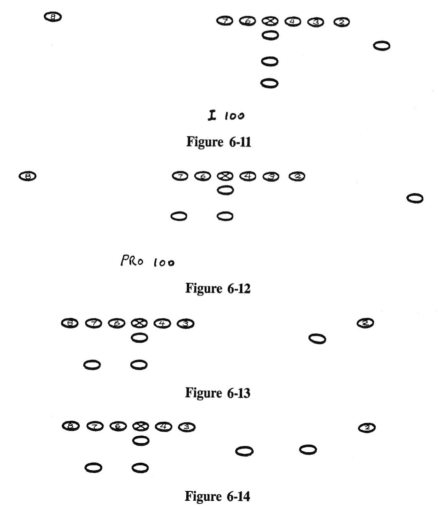

I 100

Figure 6-11

PRo 100

Figure 6-12

Figure 6-13

Figure 6-14

5. Quads—Places two wingbacks and a flanker to the side of the spread end (Figure 6-15).

Formations can be adjusted with extended motion also. There are two types of extended motion used in a Wing-T system, wingback motion and diveback motion. Wingback motion is labeled "Run to," which means that the wingback runs to the ball, going between the quarterback and fullback or "Run away," which means the wingback runs away from the ball forming a "Pro set" (Figure 6-16). Diveback motion is labeled "Motion to," which means the diveback goes in motion to the ball, going between the quarterback and fullback or

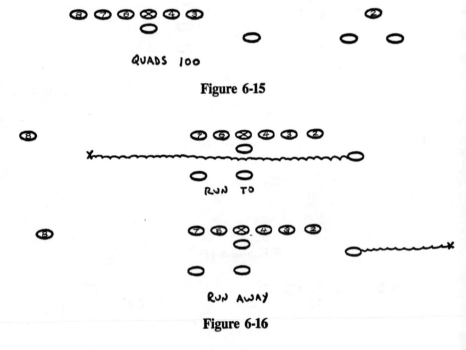

QUADS 100

Figure 6-15

RUN TO

RUN AWAY

Figure 6-16

"Motion away," which means the diveback goes in motion away from the ball (Figure 6-17).

Formations can be changed at the line of scrimmage four different ways:

1. "Slide to"—the halfbacks line up opposite the position they want to be in. An example of this would be "Slide to" 100. The left

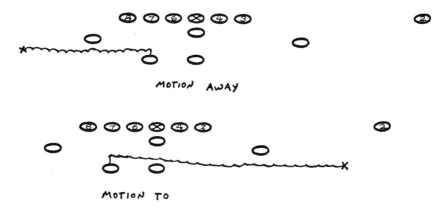

Figure 6-17

halfback would line up as a wing and move to the dive spot, while the right half would line up in the dive spot and move to the wing. This would begin as Spread 900 and change to 100 (Figure 6-18).

2. "Jump to"—Only one halfback moves with the command "Jump to," which changes the set to a double wing formation. An example of this is "Jump to" Red. The backs set up in a wing right (100) and the left half moves to the wing position, forming a tight end and wing to the right and a spread end and wing to the left (Figure 6-19).

3. "Shift to"—Both the halfbacks and ends change with the command "Shift to." An example of this would be "Shift to" 100. The tight end would begin on the left side while the spread end would begin on the right side. The left halfback would begin at the wing and the

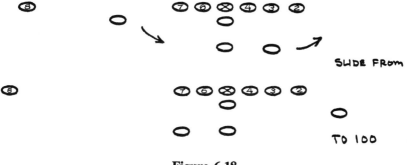

Figure 6-18

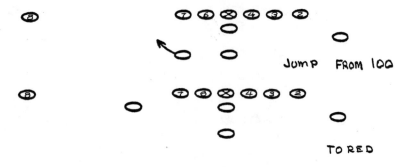

Figure 6-19

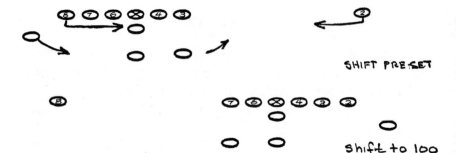

Figure 6-20

right halfback would begin in the dive spot. All four players would change going from Wing left (900) to Wing right (100) (Figure 6-20).

4. "Flip to"—The tight end begins in the fullback position and the spread end begins on the side he wants to end up on. The backs line up opposite the spread end. If, for example, the spread is on the right side, the fullback would adjust left to the dive spot and the left halfback would line up as an end on the left side. The right halfback would line up in his normal dive position. An example of this would be "Flip to" Right 100 (Figure 6-21).

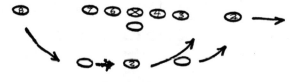

Figure 6-21

Figure 6-21 (continued)

Backfield Series

The second digit indicates the series or pattern of the backfield, which in turn assigns the ball carrier and the type of blocking. There are nine series that may be used within the Wing-T system, each of which may be run to or away from the wing. The nine series are:

1. Teen Series—a passing series in which the quarterback threatens the flank by sprinting out (Figure 6-22).

2. 20 Series—the buck sweep series in which the fullback dives up the middle and the halfbacks run at the flank (Figure 6-23).

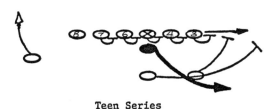

Teen Series

Figure 6-22

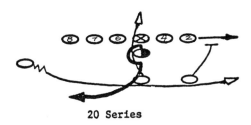

20 Series

Figure 6-23

3. 30 Series—The power series that has all the running backs going toward the point of attack (Figure 6-24).

4. 40 Series—the inside veer series that has the fullback diving for the outside foot of the attack side guard (Figure 6-25)

5. 50 Series—a passing series that has the quarterback setting up with a three-, five-, or seven-step drop behind the attack side guard (Figure 6-26).

6. 60 Series—a passing series designed to look like the 20 series (Figure 6-27).

7. 70 Series—a drop back passing series (Figure 6-28).

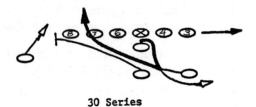

30 Series

Figure 6-24

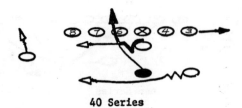

40 Series

Figure 6-25

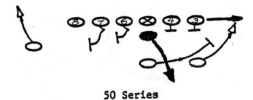

50 Series

Figure 6-26

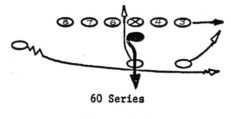

60 Series

Figure 6-27

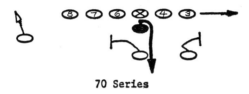

70 Series

Figure 6-28

8. 80 Series—the belly series that has the fullback running off tackle or the quarterback faking to the fullback and either passing or running the option (Figure 6-29).

9. 90 Series—a lead option series in which the quarterback fakes a 50 series pass and then goes down the line to pitch to the flaring fullback (Figure 6-30).

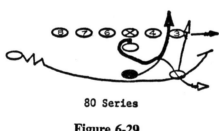

80 Series

Figure 6-29

90 Series

Figure 6-30

Point of Attack

The third and last digit is the point of attack. There are nine points of attack numbered from right to left. With the exception of the two flank areas, the holes are numbered over the seven offensive lineman (Figure 6-31). The last digit not only indicates the point of attack but assigns the man who is the primary blocker and the direction of the flow of the backfield (Figure 6-32).

The suffix that follows the third digit modifies the play by adjusting the quarterback's action, describing a pass pattern, or describing a line blocking scheme.

1. Quarterback action: Bootleg, Keep pass, Option, and Waggle.

2. Pass Routes

a. Spread end, Out, Weave, Fly, Flag, In, Post, Curl, Slant, and Hitch.

b. Tight end, Seam, Hook, Cross, Deep Cross, Drag, and Waggle.

c. Backs: Flat, Flare, Fly, Cross, Hook, and Drag.

3. Line blocking schemes: Counter, Down, Gut, J-Gut, Load, Odd, Trap, On, and Reach.

NUMBERING

Figure 6-31

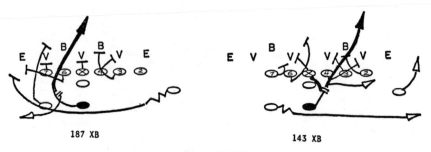

187 XB   143 XB

Figure 6-32

Starting Signal or Cadence

The starting signal is designed to facilitate the best possible takeoff for the Wing-T. In addition to giving both a rhythmic and a nonrhythmic cadence, it provides a call for shifting, a signal for a back to go in motion, and an opportunity to select a play at the line of scrimmage.

All shifting or extended motion will begin with a call of SET. The quarterback then begins a rhythmic cadence by labeling the defense with a call of *odd, even,* or *gap set,* followed by *Red (pause) Set Go.* The ball may be snapped on sound, set, or go. When extended motion is used, the ball is snapped on Red.

The play may be changed at the line of scrimmage by a calling a play and its mirror in the huddle. (Automatic 121 or 129). The quarterback directs the play right by calling *even set* or left by calling *odd set.*

OFFENSIVE SUMMARY

The Wing-T has been designed to be simple in its execution, but multiple in the problems it presents to the defense. The simplicity is accomplished by executing a relatively small number of blocking schemes. The multiplicity occurs when these blocking schemes are utilized by the three primary series and run from several formations.

In spite of the fact that there are nine points of attack numbered, there are really only three attack areas: outside, off tackle, and up the middle. These may be hit directly or with misdirection.

Almost every play in the offense is established by blocks in at the hole and out at the hole, creating a running alley. The last digit of the play number indicates not only the point of attack, but the player who blocks down if the spacing permits. If the spacing does not permit this block, the play moves inside one man via the rule assignments creating a "short" hole.

OUTSIDE GAME

The outside game consists of blocked flanks, option flanks, and quarterback bootlegs (waggles). With blocked flanks, the tight end and/or halfback will block 3 while the fullback or near guard will block out on 4. When running a blocked flank to the spread end, the spread end will follow his option blocking rule. There are five basic flanks that can be blocked: 1. To a TE and WB. 2. To a SE and WB. 3. To a TE and DB. 4. To a SE and DB and 5. To unbalanced.

1. To a tight end and wingback: 121 - Down Blocking, 182 Down Option - Down Blocking, 131 - On Blocking, (Figure 7-1).

2. To a spread end and wingback: SPR 121 - Down Blocking, SPR - 131 - On Blocking (Figure 7-2).

3. To a tight end and diveback: SPR 921 - Down Blocking (Figure 7-3).

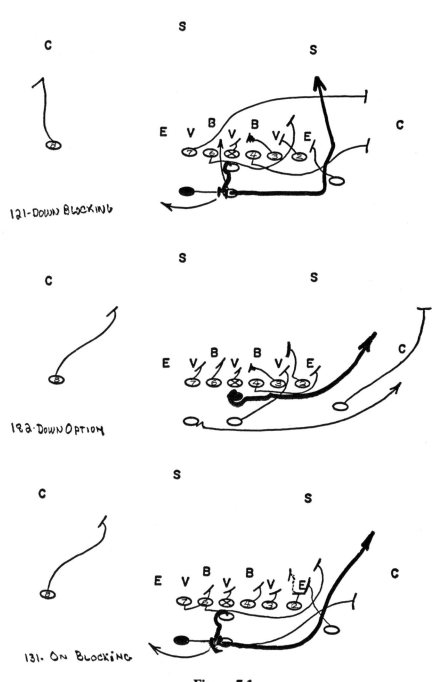

121-DOWN BLOCKING

182-DOWN OPTION

131. ON BLOCKING

Figure 7-1

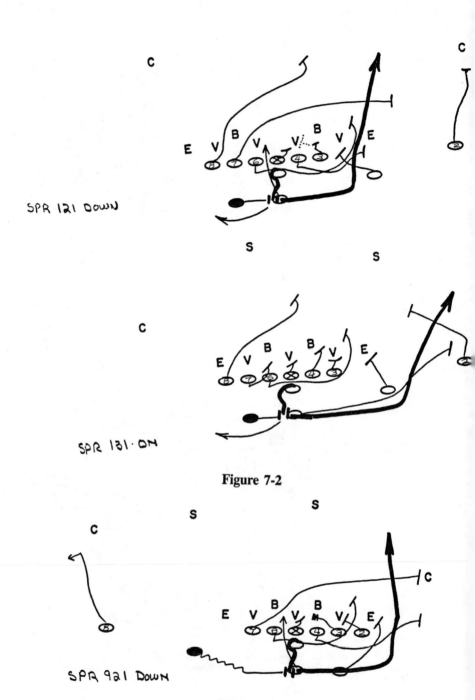

SPR 121 DOWN

SPR 131·ON

Figure 7-2

SPR 921 DOWN

Figure 7-3

4. To a spread end and diveback: 921 - Down Blocking, Split 931 - On Blocking (Figure 7-4).

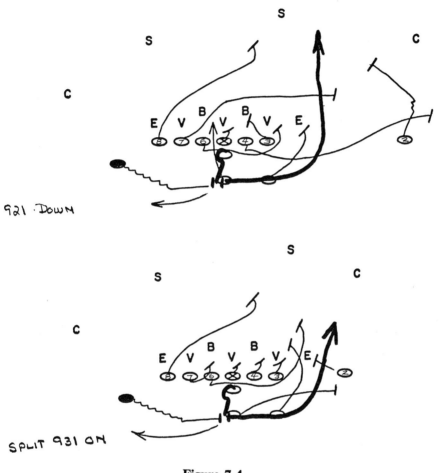

Figure 7-4

5. To unbalanced: Right 121 - Down Blocking, Right 931 - On Blocking (Figure 7-5).

The option game is run from four series: (1) 20, Trap Option, (2) 30, Option Wall, (3) 80, Belly Option, and (4) 90, Lead Option. With the basic option, the quarterback options 3, and the end and halfback block either 4 or 5 depending on the formation. Although the backfield action is different in each series the blocking at the flank is consistent.

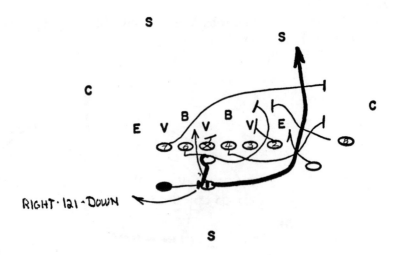

RIGHT·121-DOWN

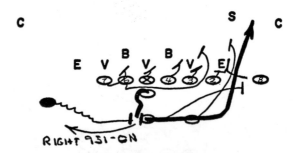

RIGHT 931-ON

Figure 7-5

1. Spread End Flank: The outside man cracks 4 (if 4 is on the line of scrimmage, he stalks 5 instead); the inside man flares and blocks the support (Figure 7-6).

2. Tight End Flank (Also Split and Slot): The outside man stalks 5 while the inside man flares and blocks the support (Figure 7-7).

3. Option Release: An adjustment in the blocking where both men release outside and look for a pass (Figure 7-8).

4. Option Load: An adjustment in the blocking where the halfback blocks 3, the end stalks 5 and the quarterback options 4 (Figure 7-9).

The bootleg (Waggle) game has the quarterback faking a handoff of a basic play and keeping in the opposite direction. With the term

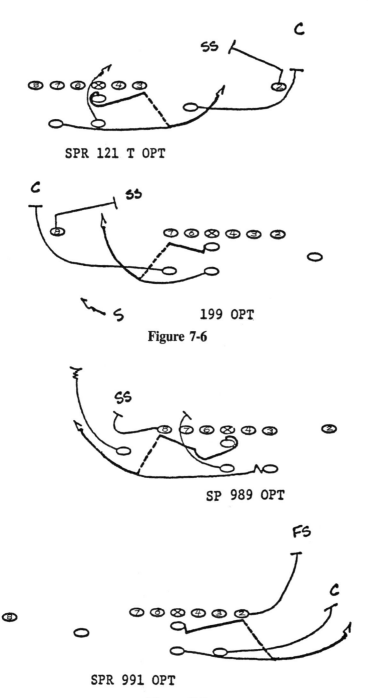

SPR 121 T OPT

199 OPT

Figure 7-6

SP 989 OPT

SPR 991 OPT

Figure 7-7

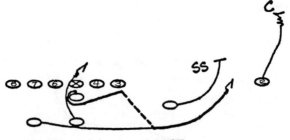

SPR 121 T OPT RELEASE

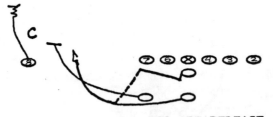

199 OPT RELEASE

Figure 7-8

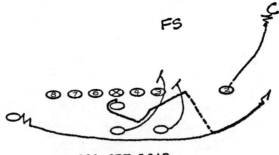

SP 981 OPT LOAD

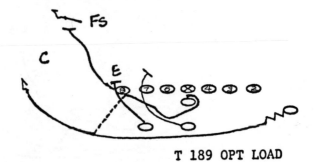

T 189 OPT LOAD

Figure 7-9

bootleg, the line blocks exactly as the run being faked, while the term waggle tells the guards to pull and block for the quarterback. The plays are: SPR 929 WAGGLE, 929 WAGGLE, 929 BOOTLEG, 936 CT. BOOTLEG (Figure 7-10).

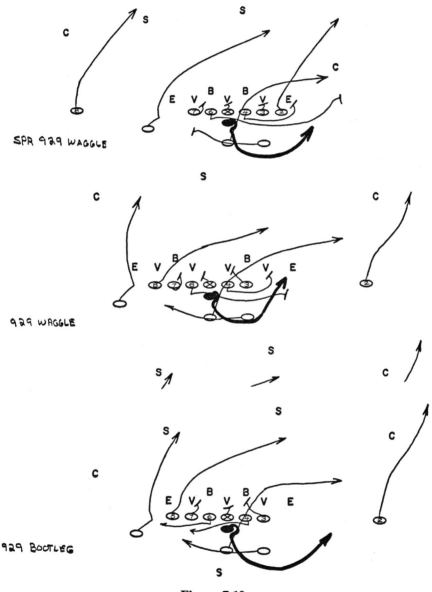

Figure 7-10

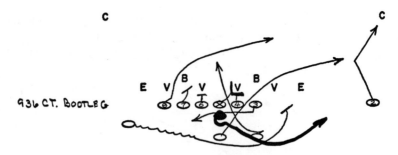

Figure 7-10 (continued)

OFF TACKLE GAME

There are two areas of attack involved in the off tackle game, the two and eight holes and the three and seven holes. The two and eight holes are run primarily to the tight end because he is primary blocker. It is possible, however, to run a two- or eight-hole play to the split end against an even defense creating a short hole. A short hole would have the three or seven man become the lead blocker. There are three primary plays run at two and eight holes, using the 80, 20, and 30 series: 182 Down, 122 Gut, and 132 (Figure 7-11)

By using 32 blocking, three misdirection shots are run away from the wing: SPR 936 ct at 2, SPR 929 Wag Shuffle at 2, SPR 932 ct XX (Figure 7-12).

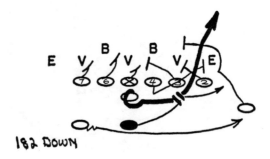

Figure 7-11

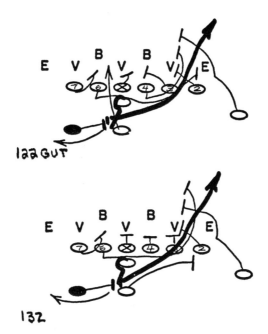

122 GUT

132

Figure 7-11 (continued)

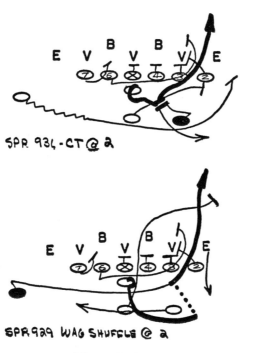

SPR 936 - CT @ 2

SPR 929 WAG SHUFFLE @ 2

Figure 7-12

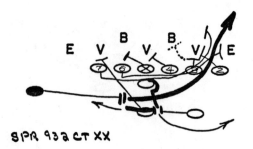

SPR 93 2 CT XX

Figure 7-12 (continued)

The three and seven hole have two direct shots from the 80 and 20 series and one misdirection from the 30 series.

The direct action shots are: 187 XB, 187 Gut, 187, SPR 123 Gut G.T., 123 G.T. to LH (Figure 7-13).

The mis-direction play is: 137 ct XX (Figure 7-14).

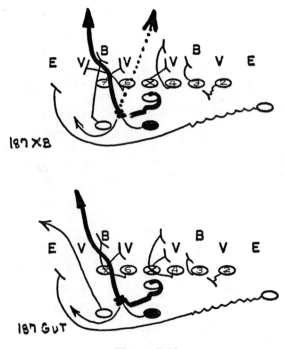

187 XB

187 GUT

Figure 7-13

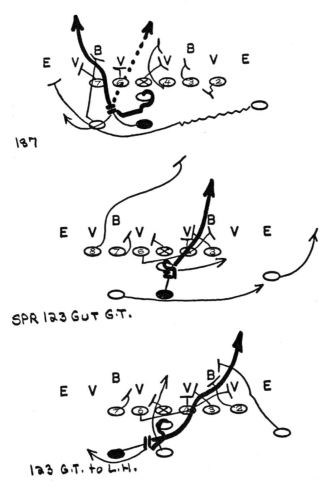

187

SPR 123 GUT G.T.

123 G.T. to L.H.

Figure 7-13 (continued)

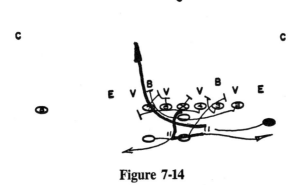

Figure 7-14

INTERNAL GAME

The plays up the middle include both direct shots and counter plays. The direct shots are run from the 20 series and employ four types of blocking. Normal, Guard Trap, Gut, and On: 24, 24 G.T., 24 Gut, 24 On (Figure 7-15).

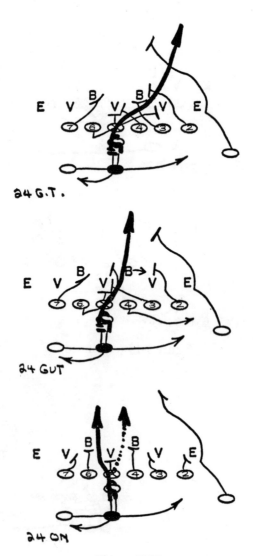

Figure 7-15

The counter plays are run from the 30 series and employ three types of blocking, Tackle Trap, Gut, and Short: 134 ct, 134 ct Gut, 134 ct Short (Figure 7-15).

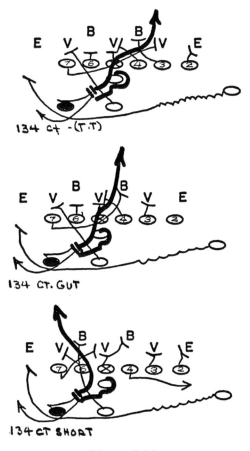

Figure 7-16

These counter plays can also be run to the wingback. The 934 ct is an example of this (Figure 7-17).

PASSING GAME

The passing game is divided into three categories: (1) keep passes and sprint out, (2) waggle or bootleg, and (3) dropback.

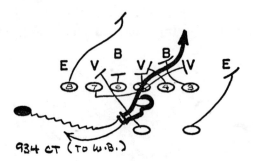

934 CT (TO W·B.)

Figure 7-17

Keep Passes and Sprint Out

The keep passes are thrown from the 80 series and are divided into two categories: (1) Basic keep pass. The quarterback threatens the flank and runs or throws depending on the support. The blocking is designed to look like run, blocking down with the tackle and pulling the guard. The pattern is a seam by the tight end and flat by the halfback (Figure 7-18). (2) Keep pass—called pattern. When a pattern other than seam and flat is used it must be called, using a suffix, in the huddle. The protection changes to *gap-on-area* to the playside and the quarterback pulls behind the playside guard at a depth of eight yards (Figure 7-19).

The sprint out also uses the seam and flat pattern, but the pass protection changes to *fire-on-area* (Figure 7-20).

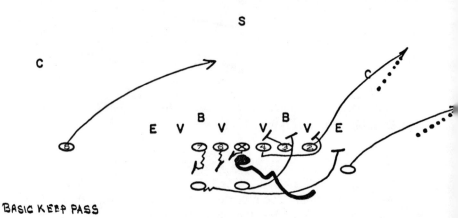

BASIC KEEP PASS

Figure 7-18

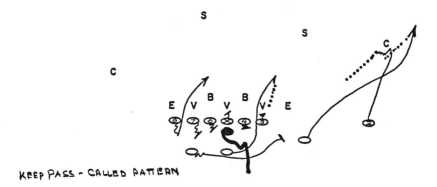

KEEP PASS - CALLED PATTERN

Figure 7-19

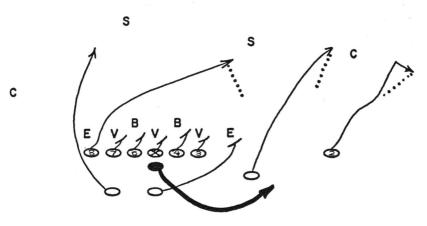

Figure 7-20

Waggle or Bootleg

The waggle is run from both the 20 series and the 80 series. When running the 20 waggle, both guards pull and the quarterback threatens the flank. The basic pattern has an end deep outside, the fullback in the flat, and a crossing man (Figure 7-21). The pattern can be adjusted by using the term "switch." The switch pattern places the fullback up the seam and the end runs an out pattern (Figure 7-22). The 60 series is used to change the line blocking so that the quarterback can pull up in order to throw back or throw inside (Figure 7-23).

The 80 Waggle is used to employ misdirection patterns from the 80 Keep Pass. The offside guard pulls and blocks at the flank (Figure 7-24).

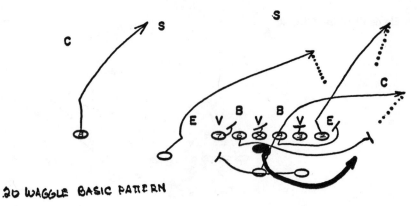

20 WAGGLE BASIC PATTERN

Figure 7-21

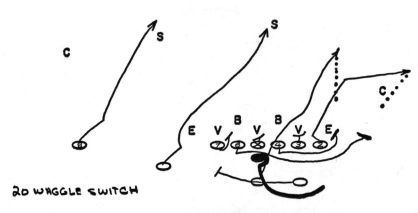

20 WAGGLE SWITCH

Figure 7-22

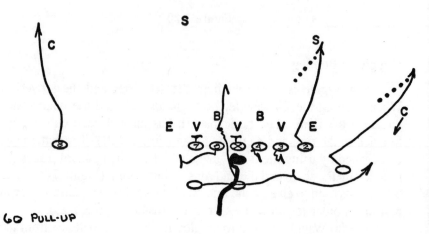

60 PULL-UP

Figure 7-23

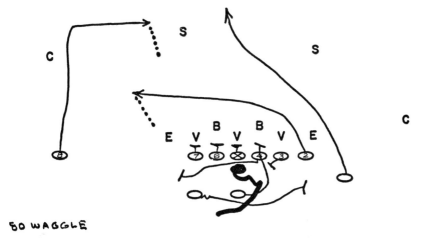

50 WAGGLE

Figure 7-24

The term Bootleg means that the quarterback will keep the ball away from the point of attack while the line will block the normal running play (Figure 7-25).

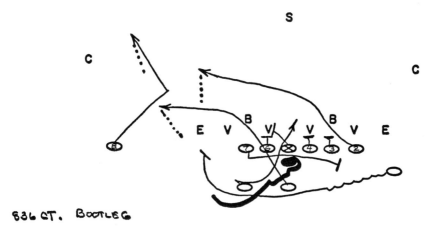

536 CT. BOOTLEG

Figure 7-25

Dropback

The Wing-T dropback protection is the same as keep pass, called pattern protection. This is done in order to reduce the teaching and drilling time for pass protection. The quarterback sets up with either a three-, five-, or seven-step drop. The depth of the drop depends on the pattern. A quick out, for example, has a three-step drop, while the curl has a seven-step drop. As with any dropback package, the Wing-T dropback has almost endless possibilities. There are, however, a few patterns that are successful and fit into the total Wing-T system.

Spread 151

The quarterback will back out three steps, read the strong corner, and throw the eight yard out to the spread end. If the strong corner rolls up to cover the out, the quarterback throws the ball to the wingback or reads the weakside. When going to the weakside, the quarterback will shuffle back two additional steps and read the inside backer. If the backer drops, the ball is dumped to the left halfback; if the drop is late or shallow, the quarterback will throw to the tight end (Figure 7-26).

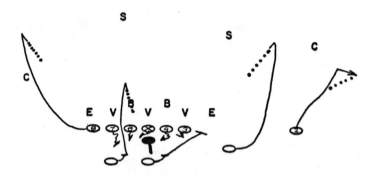

SPR 151

Figure 7-26

951 Curl

The quarterback drops seven steps and reads the outside backer. If the backer rushes, the ball is thrown to the spread end; if the backer drops, the ball is thrown to the right halfback flaring. The quarterback can go back to the offside tight end or wingback if he doesn't like the curl or flare (Figure 7-27).

Run to Blue 51 Post, Fly and Flat

The quarterback takes a five-step drop and looks to hit the post just as the spread end breaks. If the post is covered, he looks to the fly or the flat. When the secondary makes a strong "trips" adjustment, the quarterback will go back to the tight end (Figure 7-28).

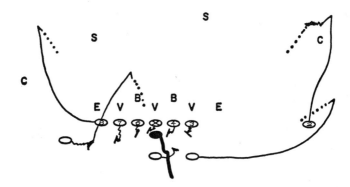

951 CURL

Figure 7-27

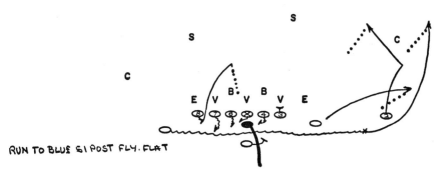

RUN TO BLUE 51 POST FLY. FLAT

Figure 7-28

OFFENSIVE GLOSSARY

Area Block	Blocking an area after taking one step forward
Away Block	Block away from the point of attack
Backer	A defensive man positioned off the line of scrimmage in a two-point stance.
Bootleg	QB keeps the ball in the opposite direction of offensive call and executes run or pass option
Bumplead	An adjustment to lead blocking where the read up aspect of the block is emphasized
Check Block	Fill for pulling man and protect that zone.
Counter	Backs run opposite to the called play with exception of the ball carrier, who runs to the point of attack.

Crack Block	Block first man inside off line of scrimmage.
Cut Off Block	Block downfield at closest point where you will intercept the defender's path to the ball carrier.
Down Block	Block first man inside.
Drag	A delayed pass cut into an open.
Drop	Step up with inside foot to check for firing backer. If backer does not fire, step to outside with depth and pivot block outside rush.
Fire Block	Aggressively block attack side gap.
Gap Block	Block man in your inside seam.
Gut Block	Step around tail of primary lineman—wall off.
Inside-out Block	Pulling lineman blocks out on first free man at point of attack.
J-Gut	Step around tail of primary lineman—log block.
Keep Pass	QB keeps the ball in the direction of the offensive call and executes run or pass option
Lead	The block that establishes an opening as in post-lead, and includes a read down responsibility.
Load	An adjustment to option blocking where the man closest to 3 blocks him while the other man stalks 5.
Log Block	Pull toward point of attack with depth, attempting to get head outside and hook defensive man. If man opens up, kick him out.
Odd Block	Backside adjustment of on block for odd defense where guard blocks outside and tackle guts inside.
Option	QB executes option of one of two alternatives, keep or pitch.
Post	The inside block of a double team where the blocker protects his inside seam after contact with the defensive man.

Post-Lead-Block	Block where defensive man is moved laterally by two offensive men.
Pull Check	Get inside position, then block-gap-on-outside.
Reach Block	Step laterally toward point of attack, then block as assigned. May exchange assignments with adjacent man on call.
Read Up	Step to block down, if defensive man on adjacent man stunts away, block backer.
Seam	Zone between two adjacent offensive linemen.
Shadow	Adjustment to reach blocking vs. odd defense, where tackle blocks, gap, on. Guard steps laterally to read backer and blocks him. Pull if he scrapes, block on if he fills.
Slam Release	Adjustment to waggle release when man is in TE's gap. The TE blocks the gap for one count, keeping his head outside in order to release freely into the pattern.
Stalk	Release off the line with speed to drive the defensive back off the line. As the DB relinquishes his cushion, come under control and maintain your position between him and the ball carrier. Under no circumstances should you permit the DB to support through you.
Tight Man	Last man on the line of scrimmage of the formation.
Waggle	Bootleg play with guard and guards pulling opposite the offensive call, protecting QB.
Wall Off Block	Block defensive pursuit at a point immediately beyond line of scrimmage.
Weave	End's release, moving with width after 4 yards of depth, reading defense.

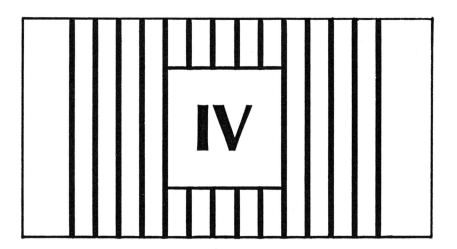

IV

COACHING
POSITION
TECHNIQUES

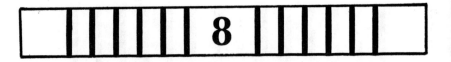

THE QUARTERBACK

No game is quite as demanding as football, and no position in football demands as much from a player as does quarterback. There are physical and mental demands placed on the quarterback and both are important. This chapter deals with the physical aspects of the position and the mental aspects will be discussed in Chapters 4, 5, 14 and 15.

STANCE

The quarterback's stance should be a neutral one that should enable him to move quickly in several directions. His assignments will require him to sprint out in either direction, reverse pivot on either foot, or back peddle away from the line. His stance begins with his feet about a foot apart, with the weight shifted slightly toward the balls of his feet. He bends at the waist as he reaches to place his hands under the center, leaving the knees slightly flexed.

TEACHING THE HANDUP

We teach the hand up using the following technique. The quarterback places the ball at the center's tail in the exact position he will expect to receive the snap. He takes the ball with his right hand on the near half of the ball, extending the majority of the ball between the right thumb and index finger, very much the way left-handed first baseman would take the ball in the webbing of his glove. With the ball in this position, he turns his hand so that the palm of his right hand faces the ground. A line between the thumb and little finger of the right hand is parallel to the line of scrimmage. This turns the long axis of the ball slightly and becomes part of a natural turn of the center's snap. He then places the thumb of his left hand along the thumb of his right hand, with the first knuckle of the left near the second of the right thumb and draws the fingers of the left hand away from the ball. The ball will be controlled initially by the right hand with the left hand in position as an insurance factor.

The center assumes his offensive stance and the quarterback places the ball under the center at the spot of the snap, placing pressure under the center's tail with the back of his right hand. The center places his right hand on the ball and removes it about a foot from the quarterback's hands and then replaces it in the quarterback's right hand. The quarterback's fingers should be relaxed as he accepts the ball into his right hand alone. The center then repeats this procedure, increasing the distance of the snap until it comes from the ground. During this practice the quarterback will coach the center with respect to the position of the ball at the snap. The center pulls the ball into position with a relativly firm elbow as opposed to swinging it. Finally the center uses both hands for the snap from his offensive stance.

CONTROL OF THE BALL

As the quarterback receives the ball from the center, his right hand rotates it a quarter of a turn to the right, and his left hand slides onto the ball. Now he has the ball at the thick part with his hands on either side. With the ball held in this position, the quarterback draws it quickly to his belt. The ball is now point first at his belt with the long axis parallel to the ground. The ball remains at his belt until he fakes with it or hands it off. It is then ready to be snapped into the carrier's hands.

REVERSE PIVOT

The quarterback will reverse pivot away from the center on many plays. The technique is consistent for all pivots, but each play requires a specific placement of the foot opposite the pivot foot, i.e., first step. As the ball is snapped into the right hand, the weight is shifted to the heel of the pivot foot. As the ball is being drawn to the belt, the head, shoulders, and hips begin the pivot in that order ahead of the feet. He should be able to see where he is moving before the step is completed. The first step of all reverse pivots is made with respect to an imaginary "mid-line" that runs perpendicular to the line of scrimmage directly through the quarterback.

The quarterback's posture, being flexed at the waist, creates natural concealment of the ball and is one of two reasons for the ball being drawn to the waist. The other is that he doesn't want the ball to swing away from his body increasing the possibility of a fumble. His elbows should remain close to his body to complete protection and the hiding of the ball.

Step Out—Step Back

The narrow stance of the quarterback enables him to step out quickly to either side or drop back. As he accepts the hand up and draws the ball to his belt, he shifts the weight to one foot and steps in the required direction with the other.

Belly (983)

The quarterback reverse pivots on his right foot. The left is placed just across the midline. The right foot then crosses over and steps toward the fullback's belly path, (about forty-five degrees from the line). Just as this step is made, the ball is quickly jabbed, using both hands, into the fullback's belly, initiating a ride. The quarterback's third step parallels the fullback's path as the ride with the ball is made. He then pulls the inside handout and pressures the ball to the fullback's belly with the outside hand. Remember, the ball is brought quickly to the quarterback's waist and then jabbed to the fullback's hand. He then steps back toward original ride depth, pulls hands to imaginary ball, and fakes the keep pass.

Buck Sweep Right (121)

The quarterback reverse pivots cleanly on his right foot. The left foot is placed on the midline as he sprints away from the center. His back is turned to the point of attack and the ball is well hidden. He then moves on the midline another step. The fullback must avoid him. The ball should be kept tight to the belt as the quarterback and fullback pass each other with the fake resulting from the speed and proximity of the two. He moves toward the left half on his third step and snaps the ball into the left half's handoff pocket at forearm length from his body. The quarterback and left half are close. Their shoulders should brush. After handing the ball off, the quarterback bends his path with both hands on an imaginary ball at his hip and fakes the bootleg at a depth of no greater than six yards. The quarterback should look to see if the free safety is pursuing the play. This will help him read when running the waggle.

Fullback Trap (124, G.T., ON, GUT)

When the fullback carries the ball up the middle on the buck sweep series, he controls the midline. The quarterback's reverse pivot is now made with respect to even or odd spacing. If there is a defensive man on the center, the quarterback will reverse pivot across the midline (one foot), enabling the fullback to dive directly for the right hip of the center. If there is no one on the center, the reverse pivot will be on the midline, giving the fullback a straight shot at the center's left hip.

The quarterback should be very conscious of pulling the ball to his belt so as not to attract linebacker attention to the ball, then pop the ball into the fullback's handoff pocket. The quarterback's back is always turned away from the point of attack. He should move toward the fullback in his second step as the handoff is made. He fakes the sweep first and then the bootleg. Care should be made not to let either hand drag away from the body. As soon as the handoff is made, the empty hand should be snapped back to an imaginary ball.

Waggle (129 Waggle)

The waggle is an option run or pass play and the quarterback must be ready to make the proper decision and be able to execute either option. The quarterback reverse pivots on his left foot and as he is moving away from the line, slides his right to take a passing grip on the ball. The quarterback takes the midline and doesn't hand fake to the fullback. On his third step the quarterback jabs a ball fake to the right half faking a sweep, then snaps the ball back to his hip (still has passing grip). The left hand is extended as though the handoff was made. The quarterback's path should be no deeper than six yards and must be executed with speed. He threatens the flank as he looks for the free safety read. If the safety flows with the halfback sweep fake, the quarterback should consider running the ball, dumping it to the fullback in the flat, or hitting the tight end in the seam. If the free safety picks up the tight end, the quarterback should look for the crossing left half.

This waggle is to a tight end flank, and the run option is apt to be good. When running the waggle to a spread end flank the quarterback must be prepared to pull up, using the back side guard's block out.

Tackle Trap (134 CT)

Once again the quarterback reads the defense. If there is a defensive man on the center, the quarterback will pivot on his left foot, placing his right foot on the midline. If there is no one on the center, this step will be just across the midline. This adjustment will enable the left half to stay close to the post-lead block. These two steps should bring him away from the center. Just as the fullback clears, the quarterback bends his path toward the handoff spot, and is prepared to snap the ball, forearm length to the handoff pocket of the left half. Then the quarterback snaps both hands back to an imaginary ball. Now fake the bootleg at no deeper than six yards so your movement will apply pressure to the defensive end.

Belly Down (182 Down)

The quarterback reverse pivots on the right foot flat and fast (180 degrees), jabs the ball into the fullback's belly on the second step, and fakes the option off his tail.

Belly Option (981 Option)

The quarterback reverse pivots flat and fast, just like the Belly Down. The quarterback should get the passing grip immediately as he pulls away from the center. As he disengages from the fullback, he should move quickly upfield to attack the inside foot of 3. He then keeps the ball or pitches to the left halfback.

Belly Keep Pass (981 KP)

The Belly Keep Pass, like the waggle, is an option run or pass play. The quarterback must, therefore, be prepared to execute either option quickly. As he is moving away from the center, he should slide his right hand forward to take a passing grip on the ball. The footwork and mesh are the same as the belly, except that the pivot is slightly flatter to enable the quarterback to get to the flank quicker. The quarterback should be ready to release the ball quickly off the fake.

Trap Option (921 Trap Option)

The quarterback reverse pivots on the right foot and steps on the midline with the left foot. The second step should also be on the midline. Both of these steps should be as short as possible and under control. On the third step the quarterback's left foot is pointed for the inside foot of 3, enabling him to get up into the line of scrimmage to execute the option. The third step should have the quarterback one yard inside of the left guard; this enables the guard to protect him from any penetration. The quarterback then keeps the ball or pitches to the left halfback.

DRILLS

Once the quarterback masters the handup and the basic pivots, which have already been discussed, he must become proficient in distributing the ball three different ways: handing off, pitching, and passing. The handoff technique for the basic plays was discussed in detail earlier in this chapter. The drills for the handoff are discussed in Chapter 9.

A.   Pitch Drills:

    1. Pitch Warmup:

        Two quarterbacks face each other at a distance of five yards by two yards. Initially they should be offset so that their right hands are to the inside. This enables them to pitch the ball to each other with their right hands. After they have finished with the right hand, they should offset the other way so that they can pitch with the left hand. The technique begins with the quarterback placing his hand on the ball in the passing grip. He then turns the hand under and flips the ball as he steps toward the target. The aiming point for the pitch should be just above the numbers, being sure to avoid a low pitch.

    2. SPR 121 TRAP OPTION - SPR 929 TRAP OPTION

        This drill is set up by having two sets of spacing boards placed as close to the center of the field as possible. The left halfbacks line up on the right side of the field and right halfbacks line up on the left side of the field. A center, half of the fullbacks, and half of the quarterbacks line up at each station. A cone is placed at the end of the spacing board to represent the inside foot of 3 and designate the "Pitch Point." Another cone is placed five yards outside the board and two yards behind the line of scrimmage. This is the point where the ball should be caught. By changing the halfbacks to the wing position, they can practice the motion pitch (Figure 8-1).

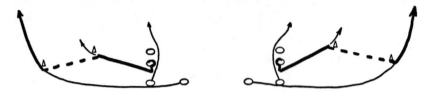

Figure 8-1

3. 981 OPTION - 189 OPTION (Belly Option)

The personnel and equipment are set up the same as for the Trap Option drill. The fullback and quarterback now execute their 82 Down technique with the quarterback pitching to the left halfback, who must leave in one step motion to get to the proper area to catch the pitch (Figure 8-2).

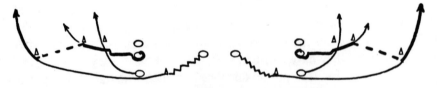

Figure 8-2

4. 991 OPTION - 199 OPTION (LEAD OPTION)

Once again the equipment remains the same, but the halfbacks change sides, i.e., the right halfbacks should be on the right side. This drill makes the fullback the pitch man and enables the halfback to practice his arc block on 4 (Figure 8-3).

Figure 8-3

B.   Throwing Drills:

1. Warmup Progression:

Two quarterbacks face each other at a depth of ten yards and throw the ball to each other. Initially, this is a loosening up process. Once the quarterbacks are loose, they should increase the distance between them to fifteen yards. At this time they should be working on their releases and throwing the ball to a particular spot, i.e., right shoulder, left shoulder and so forth. We do not believe in overcoaching the release, which could result in making the quarterback too mechanical. We want a natural, quick release without any hitches or wasted motion. By getting on top of the ball, the quarterback will be sure to have a live release. They should then simulate moving parallel to the line of scrimmage by facing the right sideline first and then the left sideline. The important part of this phase of the drill is that the quarterback must rotate his upper body so that his shoulders are square to the target when the ball is released. The warmup progression is completed by having the quarterbacks throw on the run. This is done by having the quarterback with the ball run directly at the other quarterback, who maintains the fifteen-yard separation by backpeddling. This teaches the quarterback to run directly at the target when throwing on the run.

2. Sprint Out Drill:

The most efficient drill to teach throwing on the run is the Sprint Out Drill. This drill is set up by placing cones on opposite hashes, fifteen yards apart from each other. Two quarterbacks line up at each cone. Another cone is set up at the inside foot of the halfback position. The drill is first run to the right and then, by changing hashes, to the left. The quarterback sprints around the cone at the halfback position and runs directly at the other quarterback. This ensures that he is running at the target (Figure 8-4).

3. Dropback Drill:

Four quarterbacks line up on the line of scrimmage two yards apart from each other. The tight ends and wingbacks

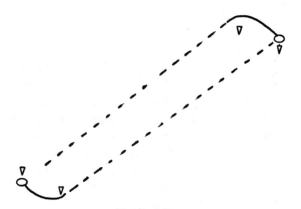

Figure 8-4

are on the right side while the split ends and divebacks are on the left side. The ends and backs change sides halfway through the drill. Each quarterback takes a five- or seven-step drop, depending on the pattern, and throws to the appropriate receiver. A good example of this is the tight end and wingback running a hook and flat combination to the right with the split end and diveback running a curl and flare combination to the left (Figure 8-5).

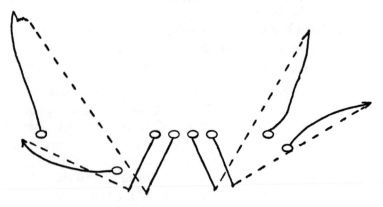

Figure 8-5

4. Belly Keep Pass Drill:

The Belly Keep Pass Drill combines the techniques of faking and throwing on the run. Two quarterbacks line up two yards apart from each other with a fullback behind each one. On the right side, the tight end and wingback line up with the split end and diveback on the left side. As with the Dropback Drill, the receivers change sides halfway through the drill. A cone is placed on the inside foot of each dive position. This forces the quarterback to get around the cone and then run directly at the target. It is extremely important that the quarterback get the passing grip immediately so that he is prepared to throw the ball quickly as he comes off the fake (Figure 8-6).

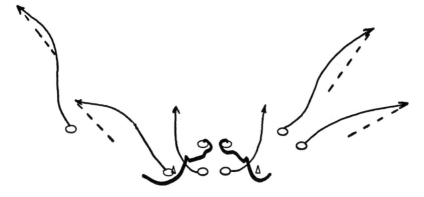

Figure 8-6

THE RUNNING BACKS

One of the positive features of the Wing-T is that it spreads the responsibility of advancing the ball through all the personnel. This makes the backfield position very interesting in that the running backs must not only master the skill of carrying the ball, but must also become adept at catching the ball, blocking, and faking.

There are two basic positions in the backfield: fullback and halfback, with the halfback broken down into wingback and diveback positions. The techniques required for all three positions are essentially the same, as is the case with the line, so the techniques described will apply to all three positions.

STANCE

The running backs use a two-point stance that enables them to move both laterally and straight ahead efficiently and precisely. Along with precision, the two-point stance enables the back to see over the offensive line in order to read the defensive spacing and coverage. This is a great advantage because it helps the back anticipate where the hole will open or what pattern adjustments should be made.

The stance begins with the feet just wider than the shoulders and the toes pointed slightly outward. The ankles, knees, and hips should be slightly flexed with the hands placed just above the knees. It is important that no weight be placed on the knees. The toes should exert pressure into the ground, placing the weight on the balls of the feet.

SHOULDER BLOCK

The backs employ the same shoulder progression as the line which is discussed in Chapter 10. The final stage of the progression is adjusted to help the back interpret the block as it relates to his position. The diveback, for example, completes the progression by running five yards before coming under control to execute the block. The wing-back lines up two yards outside and two yards deep, away from the dummy, steps with his inside foot, and delivers the blow with his head to the inside (gap block). He finishes the block by shooting the inside hand to the ground and whipping the inside leg into the dummy.

TAKEOFF

The running backs should be proficient at taking off in three directions; straight ahead, right and left, and forty-five degrees right and left. The best way to develop this takeoff is the Bird-dog drill, i.e., a one-step explosion. Once the backs have mastered the one-step explosion, they should progress to a five-yard sprint. In developing the takeoff, it is important that the coach mix up the cadence so that the players become accustomed to various snap counts.

When taking off straight ahead from the two-point stance, it is important to place more weight on the foot you want to push off. If you want to step with the left foot then more weight should be placed on the right foot. This will help eliminate any false stepping. A crossover step is preferred when going right or left, which is why the feet are placed wider than the shoulders. To get an efficient crossover step, the back should take his opposite arm (i.e., left arm when going right) and throw it tightly across the chest so that the shoulder ends up directly under the chin. This move gets the hips to rotate and facilitates the crossover step. To take off forty-five degrees to the right or to the left, the back simply takes a short lead step toward the forty-five degree target.

When the wingback goes in three-step motion, he opens up his inside hip and points his inside foot at the appropriate landmark. There are two landmarks for wingback motion; the outside foot of the diveback position for any handoff or handoff fake, and the inside foot of the original dive position for any play-action pass or option.

HANDOFF

A halfback receives the ball from the quarterback by placing his inside hand on his inside hip with the fingers pointed at a forty-five degree angle. The other hand should specifically be placed on the midline of the abdomen with the fingers pointed downward. It is very important for the inside hand to be firmly anchored to the hip to ensure a solid handoff. The quarterback executes a one-handoff, placing the ball into the halfback's inside hand at forearm's length and feathering the ball by rolling the hand over the top. This handoff enables the quarterback and halfback to get very close to each other and increases the deception of the play.

When handing off to the fullbacks, the quarterback executes a two-handed handoff that enables him to ride the ball into the fullback's belly. In order to provide a pocket for this ride, the fullback receives the ball with his inside elbow up. To ensure that the elbow is high enough, he should point his thumb downward. His other arm should be placed across the lower part of his abdomen, forming a pocket into which the ball is placed.

RUNNING GAME TECHNIQUE

The running backs have two basic responsibilities in the running game, carrying the ball and blocking. The techniques for these two responsibilities will be described separately.

1. Ball Carrying: Left Halfback
   a. 121 - Cross over and run through the fullback's position. Receive the handoff on the second step and read the right halfback's block. Make a sharp cut upfield or bounce outside depending on the support angle of 4 (Figure 9-1).

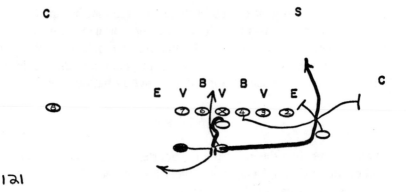

Figure 9-1

b. 921—Leave in three-step motion for the outside foot of the diveback position. Receive the handoff and execute as 121 (Figure 9-2).

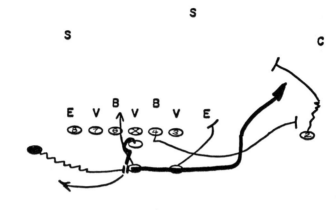

Figure 9-2

c. 182 Down Option—Leave in one-step motion and run off the tail of the fullback. Go for a point five yards outside the tight end's original position and two yards behind the line of scrimmage. This is the basic pitch position for all option plays. From this point, parallel the path of the quarterback and look for the pitch (Figure 9-3).

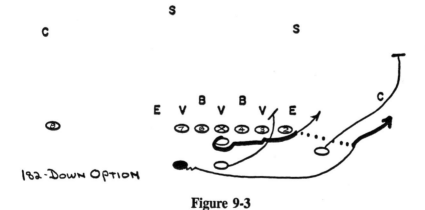

Figure 9-3

d. 981 Option Load—Leave in three-step motion for the inside foot of the diveback position. From this point, execute as 182 Down Option (Figure 9-4).

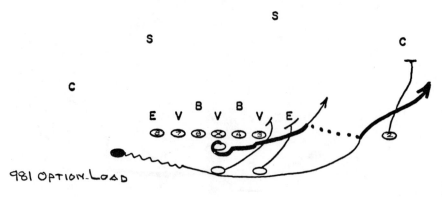

981 OPTION LOAD

Figure 9-4

e. Spread 121 Trap Option—Cross over and run through the fullback's position. Continue path to the five yard by two yard basic pitch position and then parallel to the quarterback (Figure 9-5).

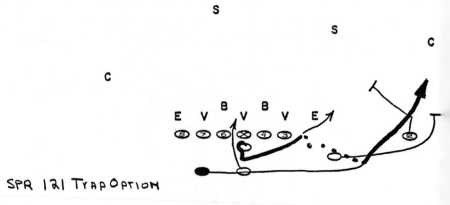

SPR 121 TRAP OPTION

Figure 9-5

f. 921 Trap Option—Leave in three-step motion for the outside foot of the diveback position. From this point execute as SPR 121 Trap Option (Figure 9-6).

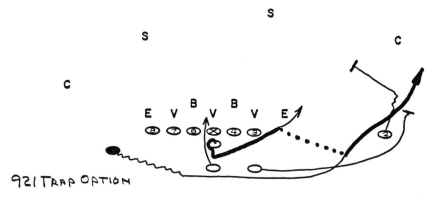

921 TRAP OPTION

Figure 9-6

g. 132—Normal Hole—Cross over for wingback's position. Receive handoff and run directly into the hole off the tail of the tight end (Figure 9-7).

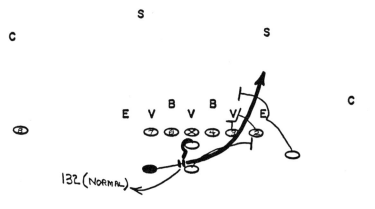

132 (NORMAL)

Figure 9-7

Short Hole—Cross over for the outside foot of the tight end. Receive the handoff and run directly into the hole off the tail of the tackle (Figure 9-8).

h. 122 Gut—Cross over for the inside foot of the tight end. Receive inside handoff and run directly into the hole off the tail of the tight end (Figure 9-9).

i. 123 Guard Trap to Left Halfback—Cross over for the inside foot of the tight end. Receive inside handoff and

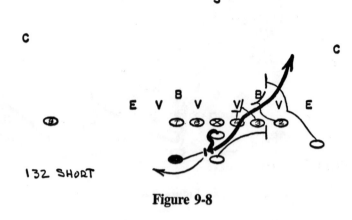

132 SHORT

Figure 9-8

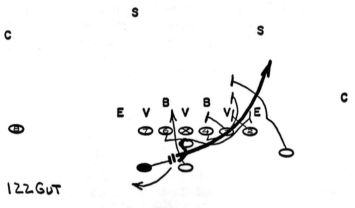

122 GUT

Figure 9-9

adjust directly into the hole off the tail of the tackle (Figure 9-10).

j. 933 Counter Criss Cross—Open up with the inside foot and get one yard of depth. Receive handoff from the right halfback over the outside foot of the left guard and head for the tail of the right guard (Figure 9-11).

k. 134 Counter—Rock weight to outside foot. Then take a lead step with the inside foot. Receive handoff on the next step and head for the tail of the center against odd spacing (left foot of center against even spacing). Stay tight to the lead post and adjust to the tackle's block on the linebacker (Figure 9-12).

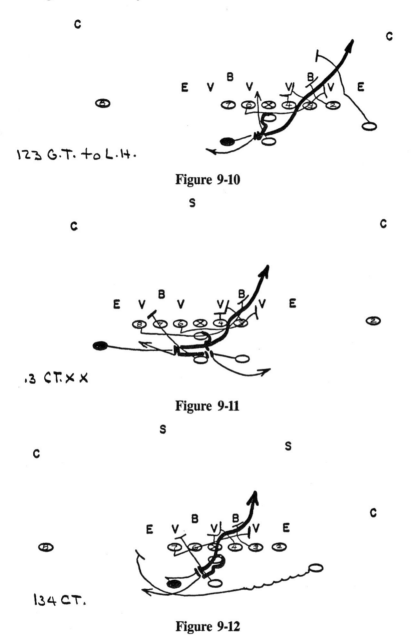

Figure 9-10

123 G.T. to L.H.

Figure 9-11

.3 CT. X X

Figure 9-12

134 CT.

1. 934 Counter—Leave in three-step motion for the outside foot of the diveback position. From this point, execute as 134 Counter (Figure 9-13).

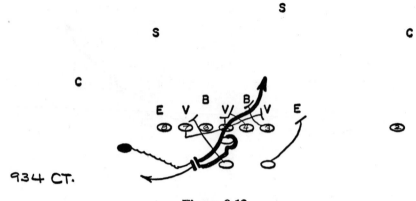

934 CT.

Figure 9-13

2. Blocking: Right Halfback
   a. 121—Step with the inside foot for the tail of the tight
   end. Block the first man to the inside, stopping penetration by getting the head across. Sustain the block by
   shooting the inside hand to the ground and whipping the
   inside leg into the hip of the man being blocked (Figure
   9-14).

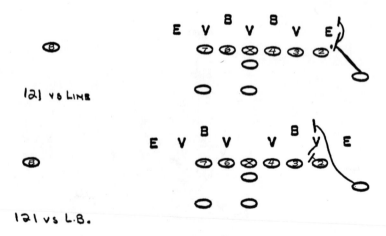

Figure 9-14

   b. 921—Run for a spot two yards outside the offensive
   tackle. Make contact with the left shoulder through the
   outside hip of the man being blocked. Block the first

man from the landmark to the inside. Prevent any penetration between the landmark and the tackle's block by adjusting the path to meet any pressure (Figure 9-15).

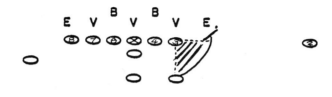

Figure 9-15

c. 131—Step upfield with the inside foot anticipating a post block from the tight end. Lead with left shoulder. Be prepared to move on to the linebacker if the man being posted disappears into the tight end's gap (Figure 9-16).

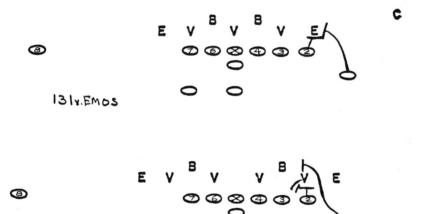

Figure 9-16

d. 981 Option—Flare for the outside foot of the split end and read the support. Stalk 5 against invert and block 4 against roll support (Figure 9-17).

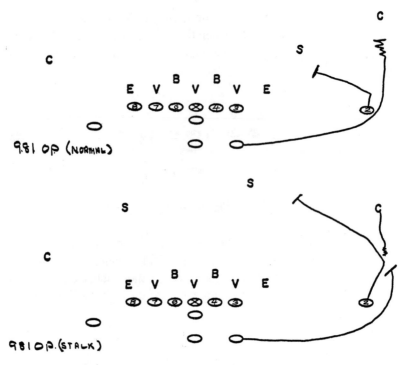

Figure 9-17

   e. 981 Option Load—Execute as 921.

   f. Spread 121 Trap Option—Flare for the outside of foot of the split end. Get a head up position on 5 and block him. Check 4 as you flare and block him if he penetrates or if he is on the line of scrimmage (Figure 9-18).

3. Ball Carrying: Fullback

   a. 124 On, Guard Trap, Gut

     1) Versus Odd—Dive for the tail of the center leading with the right foot. Receive handoff on the second step and adjust tight to the block on the nose man (Figure 9-19).

     2) Versus Even—Dive for the left foot of the center and read the defensive tackle playing over left guard (Figure 9-20).

   b. 123 Guard Trap

     1) Versus Odd—Execute as 124 Guard Trap

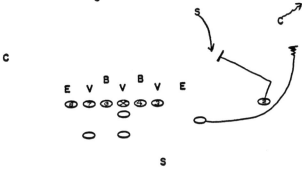

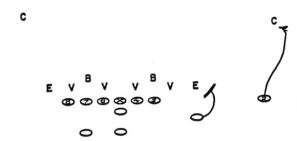

SPR 121 TRAP OPTION

Figure 9-18

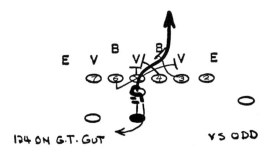

124 ON G.T. GUT   VS ODD

Figure 9-19

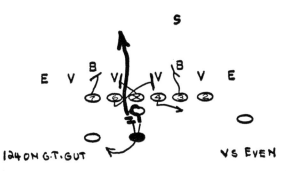

124 ON G.T. GUT   VS EVEN

Figure 9-20

2) Versus Even—Dive for the right foot of the center.
   Receive handoff on second step and adjust tightly off
   the tail of the right tackle (Figure 9-21).

Figure 9-21

c. 983 Cross Block—Take a short lead step, parallel to the
   line of scrimmage with the right foot. Cross over with
   the left foot and aim for the inside foot of the right
   tackle on the third step. Receive handoff on the third
   step and read the defensive tackle (nose man against
   Odd). Look for the windback, cutting behind the pursuit
   (Figure 9-22).

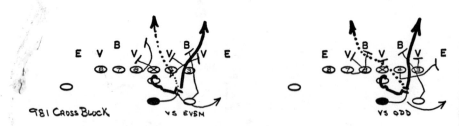

Figure 9-22

d. 182 Down, Gut—Lead step with the right foot for the
   inside foot of the tight end. Adjust path so that you cross
   the line of scrimmage over the outside foot of the tackle.
   Receive handoff on the third step and adjust tight off the
   tight end's block (Figure 9-23).
e. 991 Option—Cross over and flare to the right flank.
   Receive pitch from the quarterback at a distance of five
   yards by two yards. Adjust off of the right halfback's
   block on 4 (Figure 9-24).

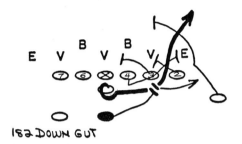

Figure 9-23

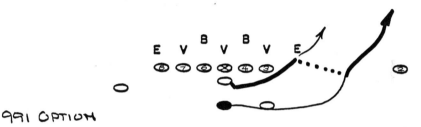

Figure 9-24

PASSING GAME TECHNIQUE

In order to simplify the passing game, the halfback has only a few routes to master. Although the number of routes used by the backs is small, their role in the passing game is very large. The halfback to the playside is normally involved in a combination pattern with the end. Seam and Flat is a good example of this (Figure 9-25).

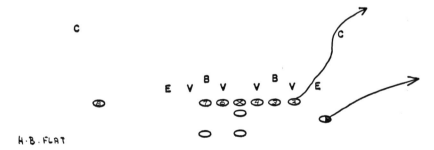

Figure 9-25

These combination patterns are designed to put two receivers into one defensive back's area. If the corner covers the seam, the flat is open. This provides the quarterback with a simple read. Curl and Fly is another example (Figure 9-26). The halfback away from the play runs either a crossing pattern or a delay pattern if he is not involved in the blocking scheme (Figure 9-27). The various patterns employed by the backs are best illustrated with the backfield route tree (Figure 9-28). The reads for the backs running crossing patterns are the same as those described for the ends in Chapter 11.

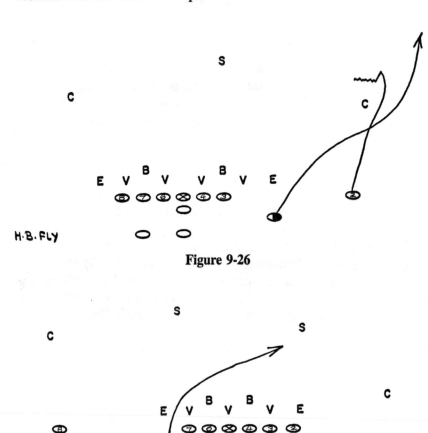

H·B· FLY

Figure 9-26

Figure 9-27

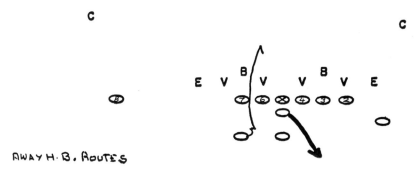

AWAY H.B. ROUTES

Figure 9-27 (continued)

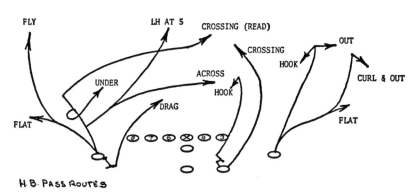

H.B. PASS ROUTES

Figure 9-28

DRILLS

The backs must be drilled in three areas: ball carrying, blocking, and pass receiving.

1. Ball Carrying:
   a. Pivot Drill: The Pivot drill is designed to teach the ball carrier to get his weight over and to accelerate into and through contact while protecting the ball. The drill is set up by placing dummies five yards apart in a diagonal pattern. The back should keep the ball in the same hand as he progresses through the dummies. He should explode into the dummy with his inside shoulder and simultaneously roll off that shoulder and head for the next dummy (Figure 9-29).

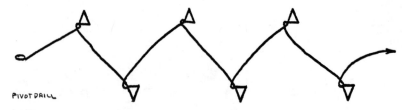

PIVOT DRILL

Figure 9-29

b. Serpentine Drill: The Serpentine drill teaches a ball carrier to make a move and still keep the ball tight to his body. The ball should be carried in the same hand throughout the drill. This drill is set up by placing dummies five yards apart in a straight line. The back runs in a serpentine path through the dummies being sure to keep the ball tight to his body (Figure 9-30).

SERPENTINE DRILL

Figure 9-30

c. Safety Angles: Safety Angles is a combination Offensive-Defensive drill that teaches the ball carrier to cut sharply upfield if the defensive back overruns the play. The left halfback runs around right end against a defensive back who is lined up five yards deep over the right guard. It is important for the ball carrier to run full speed to force the defensive back to open up in order to contain him (Figure 9-31).

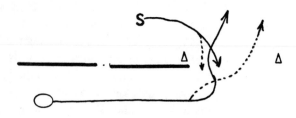

SAFETY ANGLE DRILL

Figure 9-31

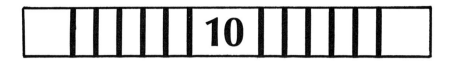

THE LINEMEN

The Offensive Line in the Wing-T is designed to develop conflicts within the blocking schemes that make it difficult for the defensive front to react quickly. In order to develop these conflicts, a number of individual techniques must be mastered and a variety of blocking schemes must be learned. Because of the complexity of these blocking schemes, Wing-T Offensive Line play is both challenging and enjoyable.

There are three basic positions within the line: Tackle, Guard, and Center. The techniques required for all three positions are essentially the same and thus the techniques described will apply to all three positions.

STANCE

A good stance is necessary to get the proper takeoff and is therefore the most fundamental technique to be mastered. The Wing-T requires that a lineman be able to move quickly in every direction and therefore a balanced stance is preferred. To attain a balanced stance, the lineman should place his feet at shoulder width with the feet pointed straight ahead. With a right-handed stance, the right foot should be moved back placing it even with the instep of the left foot. The ankle, knee, and hip joints should then be flexed so that the elbows can be placed on the knees with the back parallel to the ground. The stance is completed by extending the right arm out in front of the right eye and placing the fingers on the ground just in front of the shoulders. The left arm is flexed with the elbow comfortably placed on the left thigh.

SHOULDER BLOCK

The shoulder block is the only block used in the Wing-T for a couple of reasons. First, the shoulder is the only padded area of the body that may be used legally to strike a blow. Second, by using the proper surface, a blocker can execute the two key ingredients of a successful block, explosion and sustenance, best. The shoulder block also can be sustained best because of the large surface developed by getting the hand and arm in the proper position.

SURFACE

The blocking surface of the shoulder block extends from the sterno-clavicular joint, across the front of the shoulder, down the upper arm and back along the forearm to the fist, which is placed firmly on the near side of the chest. An individual learns this surface by placing himself in front of a large dummy on his hands and knees. From this position, he will move into a right shoulder block and then a left shoulder block, holding his block for each shoulder until he can be checked for proper body position. Both shoulders should be parallel to the ground with the shoulder slightly higher than the hips. This alignment can be attained by having both the fist, which is placed on the chest, and the front of the shoulder in contact with the dummy. The head is slid out of the way with the eyes looking up.

EXPLOSION

Explosion is then developed in three stages:

1. hands and knees on the ground
2. two-point stance
3. three-point stance

The first stage is taught from the hands and knees on ground position in order to emphasize hip explosion without getting the legs involved. This is accomplished by keeping the knees in contact with the ground throughout the explosion, which ensures that all the power is generated through the hip extension into the upper body. As the hips extend forward, the fist should be brought to the chest while the individual delivers a blow with both the forearm and shoulder. This technique is done three times with each shoulder. The three repetitions should be done rapidly with a hit, recoil, hit rhythm. The second stage is initiated from two points and is analogous to any technique in which something is thrown. An example of this would be throwing a ball. When throwing a ball with the right hand one should first step with the left foot and then throw off this foot and follow through. The same holds true when blocking with the right shoulder. The first move should be a short step (one foot) with the left foot. One addition should be added to the throwing technique and that is to simultaneously lower the center of gravity by flexing the knees. The blocker should then explode off this foot and have the entire right side of the body go through the target. It is at this point that the hip explosion should occur. As the follow through is performed, the right foot should end up well in front of the left foot. This technique is best drilled with a two-count procedure, i.e., step-pause-hit, and should be done two ways. First the blocker should do this against air, as that will force him to follow through properly. Next, he should repeat the procedure against a large dummy. The third and final stage of the explosion progression is performed from the three-point stance that is the actual playing position. In this stage, the blocker merely comes out of his stance and repeats stage two.

TAKEOFF

Once the stance and shoulder block are learned, the takeoff must be drilled to get the player to move quickly and efficiently to the target area. The drill that best teaches takeoff is called the Bird Dog Drill. It is simply a one-step explosion first with the right foot and then with the left foot. There are three directions of takeoff that the player must master:

1. right foot forward
2. right foot forty-five degrees right
3. right foot right

These three directions are repeated with the left foot. Pulling is then taught by expanding on step three. With a right-handed stance, it is easier to begin pulling right because the right foot is slightly back and out of the way. The player should put more weight on his left foot in the stance. The first step is a short step with the right foot pointed parallel to the line of scrimmage. Simultaneously, the shoulders are rotated to the right by bringing the right arm back around the trunk of the body and throwing the left arm tight across the chest. It is very important to remain low during this first step, which is taught by using the Bird Dog Drill. After the first step is mastered, the player merely runs to the designated landmark to complete the pulling technique. When pulling to the left from a right-handed stance, the player should put more weight on the right foot in the stance. The rest of the technique is executed just the opposite of pulling to the right.

INDIVIDUAL BLOCKING TECHNIQUES

After mastering these takeoff requirements, the player is ready to execute the specific blocking techniques. A Wing-T lineman must master the following individual blocking techniques (Figure 10-1).

1. right shoulder straight ahead
2. left shoulder straight ahead
3. right shoulder right
4. left shoulder left
5. gap right
6. gap left
7. fire right
8. fire left
9. reach right
10. reach left
11. trap right (inside out)
12. trap left (inside out)

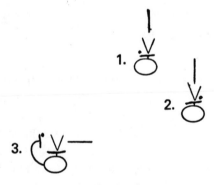

Figure 10-1

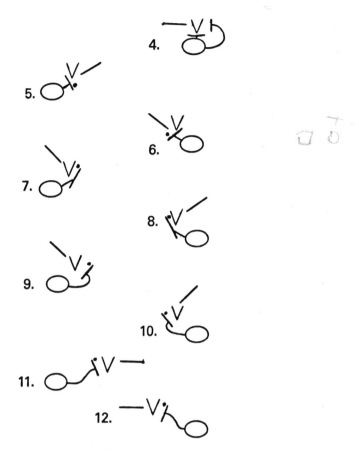

Figure 10-1 (continued)

COMBINATION BLOCKS

Two linemen are then put together to learn the following combination blocks (Figure 10-2).

1. cross block right
2. cross block left
3. gut right
4. gut left
5. lead-post right
6. lead-post left

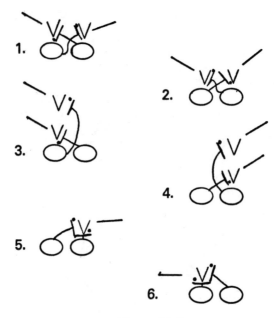

Figure 10-2

PASS PROTECTION

Wing-T pass protection is designed for both play-action and drop-back passing and thus a frontside protection that is *gap-on-area* and a backside that is *step-and-cup*. These rules are defined in the Glossary. It is important for the lineman to understand the rules for pass blocking. A blocker can use his hands as long as they remain within the confines of his body and the defensive player is in front of him. His first step should be back and inside with his inside foot in order to force an outside pass rush. It is extremely important for the blocker to remain between the passer and the rusher. As the rusher moves into him, he should deliver a blow with both hands just under the shoulder pads. As he unloads, he should give a slight amount of ground and be ready to unload again. The blocker should continue to move his feet throughout the block and be sure not to lunge at the rusher.

LINE BLOCKING TECHNIQUES

The Wing-T requires a lineman to master twelve blocking techniques:

1. Area Block—An area block is used to solidify an area on the line of scrimmage. The player should come off the ball low and firm for one step with his inside foot, then bring his other foot parallel to the original step. The feet should be slightly less than shoulder width and the center of gravity should be low. This position should be held for two counts and the player should block anyone who tries to come through his area. After the two counts, the player can take off and block anyone in front of him (Figure 10-3).

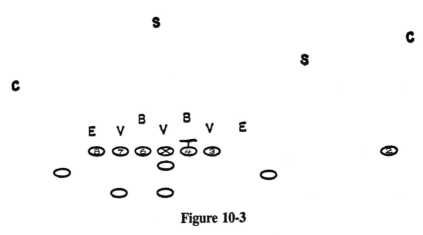

Figure 10-3

2. Bumplead—The bumplead is a combination block that is a variation of the lead-post block. The post blocker should come off the ball stronger than a normal post enabling him to eventually handle the defensive man by himself. This frees the lead blocker to move on to a linebacker after delivering a blow with his inside shoulder.

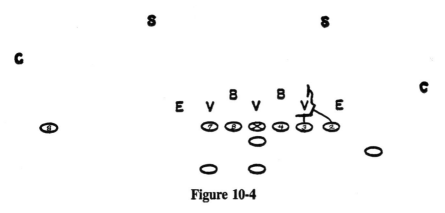

Figure 10-4

   3. Check Block—The Check Block is used to close a seam to the inside that is created when the adjacent man pulls. The first step is to the inside parallel to the line of scrimmage, which enables the player to block anyone who attempts to come through this area. If no one comes, the player should turn back and look for someone to come from the outside (Figure 10-5).

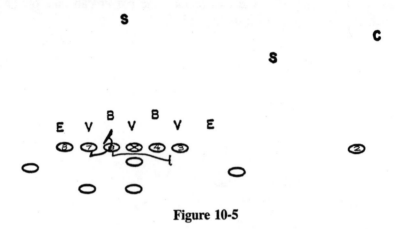

Figure 10-5

   4. Cutoff Block—The cutoff block is used to have a player who is away from the point of attack run downfield to an area where he can assist a running back in the secondary. The player should release to the inside and run downfield toward the point of attack. He should attempt to get between a defensive player and the ball carrier and then block the defensive man (Figure 10-6).

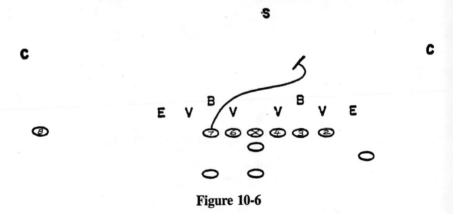

Figure 10-6

5. Down Block—The down block is used to block a defensive player who is on an adjacent lineman to the inside. The first step is to the inside in order to stop penetration. If the defensive player is not penetrating the blocker should adjust into a reverse body block by whipping his outside leg to the inside (Figure 10-7).

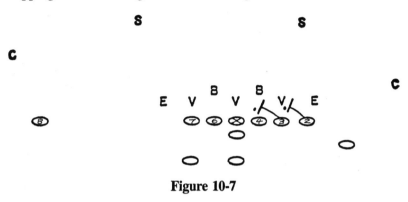

Figure 10-7

6. Fire Block—The fire block is used to establish contact with a defensive player positioned to the outside and then fight to obtain a good position to cut off the defensive player's pursuit. It is used mostly on the sweeps and options. The first step is to the outside at a forty-five degree angle to aggressively block the attack-side gap. The block is executed by aggressively throwing the inside shoulder through the defensive player's outside knee. The feet should then be accellerated and the hips should work upfield to get leverage on the defensive player (Figure 10-8).

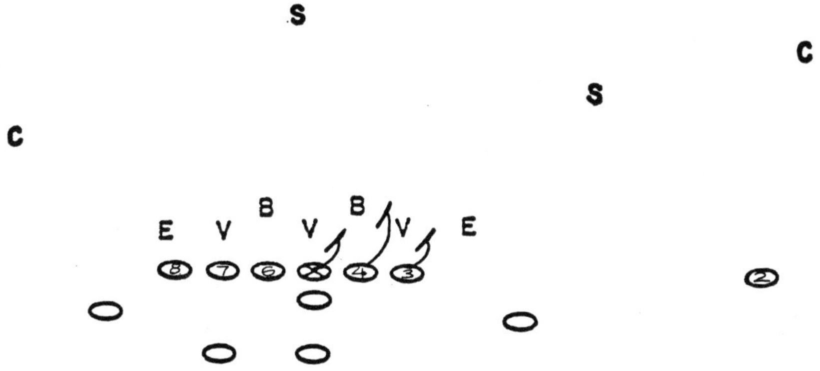

Figure 10-8

7. Gap Block—The gap block is used to cut off penetration when a defensive player is lined up in the inside gap. The first step is to the inside parallel to the line of scrimmage. The head should be placed in front to stop penetration. If no defensive player is in the gap, the blocker should move upfield to a linebacker (Figure 10-9).

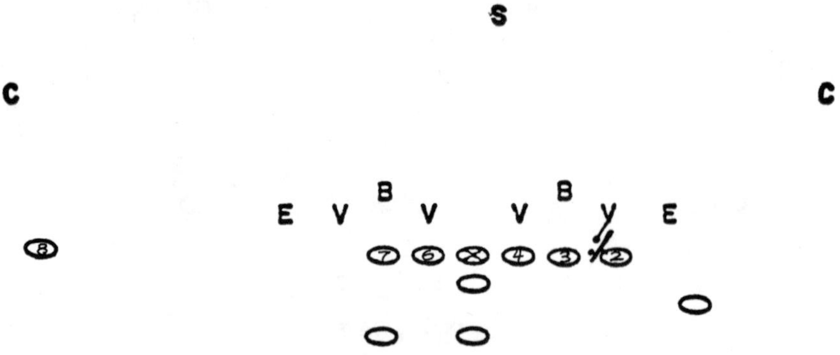

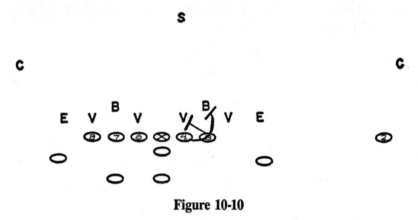

Figure 10-9

8. Gut Block—The gut block is used by a pulling lineman when it is preferable to wall off a linebacker rather than to trap a lineman. The pulling lineman will step around a down block or lead post low and tight and then move to the inside to block with his inside shoulder (Figure 10-10).

Figure 10-10

9. Inside-Out Block (Trap)—The inside-out block is used to complete a lateral opening from the inside. The player pulls to the point of attack adjusting his first step to get up into the line of

scrimmage. Contact is made with the right shoulder when going right, which puts the head on the downfield side of the player being blocked. This is accomplished by planting the downfield foot (left) and exploding through the defender (Figure 10-11).

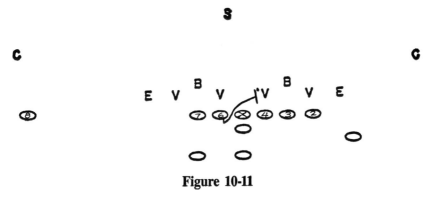

Figure 10-11

10. Lead-Post Block—The lead post is a double-team block used to establish a point of attack by having two men move one man laterally. The post man should come off the ball low with his head to the inside away from the lead blocker, taking care not to knock the defensive man off the line of scrimmage. At the moment of contact, the post man should swing his tail toward the lead blocker. The lead blocker should take a step with his inside foot and place his head away from the post man. He should then mesh tightly with the post man. Both the post and the lead must be sure to get off the ball low and quickly to prevent the defensive man from getting underneath the block and burying himself. The block is completed by driving the defensive man laterally (Figure 10-12).

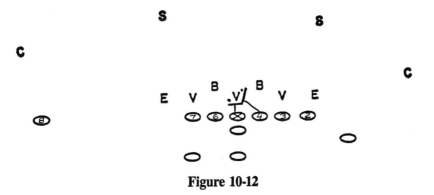

Figure 10-12

11. Log Block—The log block is used by a pulling lineman to get outside position on a defensive man who is normally trapped. The pulling lineman should pull parallel to the line of scrimmage toward the point of attack. He should deliver a blow with his inside shoulder through the outside hip of the defensive man. As he explodes through the defensive man's outside hip, he should swing his hips in order to drive upfield (Figure 10-13).

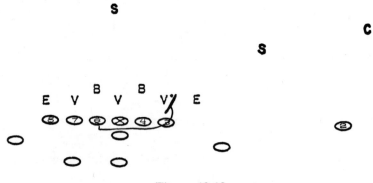

Figure 10-13

12. Reach Block—The reach block is used as a technique to adjust to defensive stunts by having the lineman step to the outside gap. The first step should be parallel to the line of scrimmage toward the point of attack. As this step is taken, the offensive lineman reads the defense and blocks whoever stunts into this area. If no one stunts, he should move upfield to block a linebacker. As with the fire block, the hips should work upfield to get leverage on the defensive player (Figure 10-14).

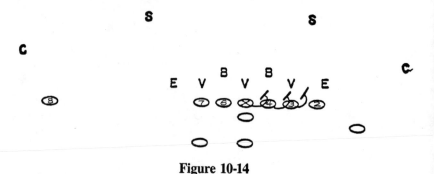

Figure 10-14

DRILLS

The combination drills used by the Wing-T lineman break down the fundamental components of the basic Wing-T plays. These drills are used to effectively get repetition with the techniques and angles that must be perfected within the Wing-T system. There are four drills and all the lineman, regardless of position, practice each drill.

1. The Waggle Drill—The waggle drill is used to teach the guards the proper path and blocking technique for the waggle. Two dummies are placed at the point of attack, one on the outside foot of the tight end and the second three yards outside the tight end and four yards deep in the offensive backfield. Two cones are also used, with the first cone placed one yard deep behind the tail of the tackle, and the second placed three yards deep behind the outside foot of the tackle. Two lineman line up in the guards' positions and execute the waggle technique for the two guards. The frontside guard pulls, getting one yard depth behind the first cone and just passed the dummy lined up on the outside foot of the tight end. He should then block back on that dummy, establishing the flank for the quarterback. The backside guard pulls with one flat step and then adjusts off the tail of the imaginary fullback getting to a depth of three yards. This will put him just inside the second cone. He then kicks out the second dummy, which is four yards deep in the backfield (Figure 10-15).

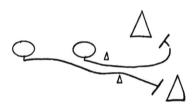

Figure 10-15

2. The Buck Sweep Drill—The buck sweep drill is used to teach the front and backside guards the proper path and blocking technique for the buck sweep. As with the waggle drill, two dummies and two cones are used. The first dummy is placed three yards outside the spacing board and two yards deep in the backfield and the second dummy is placed on the outside foot of the tackle. The first cone is placed on the outside foot of the tight end to represent the wingback's

block on the defensive end, and the second cone is placed two yards deep behind the outside foot of the tackle. The frontside guard pulls, stepping back forty-five degrees with the first step toward the second cone. On the third step the guard should level off and then adjust toward the line of scrimmage, aiming for the cone placed on the outside foot of the tight end. He should then block out on the dummy placed at the flank, getting his head to the inside. The backside guard pulls, getting slight depth, and logs the dummy on the tackle (Figure 10-16).

Figure 10-16

3. The Short Trap Drill—The short trap drill is used to teach the lead post and inside out blocks. Two dummies are used with one being placed on the center and one placed on the tackle. A center and two guards are used in this drill. The center and onside guard lead post the dummy on the center and the backside guard pulls across the center and traps the dummy over the tackle. The backside guard takes a short step with the inside foot and then adjusts tight to the lead post on the second step. This puts him in a good inside position to trap, getting his head upfield (Figure 10-17).

Figure 10-17

4. The Gut Drill—The gut drill is used to teach a lineman to pull through the hole to block a linebacker. Three dummies are used with one being placed as a linebacker over the center and one placed on each guard. The frontside guard pulls away to act as a false key. The center blocks back on the dummy lined up on the backside guard. The

backside guard pulls behind the center with a short step. On the second step the backside guard stays low and tight to the tail of the center. He then turns up through the hole and blocks the linebacker placing his head to the attack side (Figure 10-18).

Figure 10-18

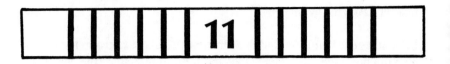

11

THE ENDS

One of the main characteristics of the Wing-T is that it is flank oriented, which makes the end positions very important. There are two distinct positions for the ends, the tight end and the split end. The tight end is a combination offensive lineman and pass receiver whereas the split end is primarily a pass receiver. Blocking is extremely important, however, to both positions.

STANCE

Because the tight end must execute many of the techniques required of the offensive lineman, his stance is similar to the lineman's (refer to Chapter 10). The only difference is that because the tight end has to sprint into the secondary when running a pass pattern, he should drop his inside foot to get a toe to heel relationship. The inside foot is dropped because the tight end always places his inside hand down. His inside hand is down because most of his blocks and releases are to the inside.

The split end's release is normally a sprint into the secondary, therefore a sprinter's stance is desirable. This places his inside foot about six inches behind his outside foot, with the width being about twelve inches. As with the tight end, the split end always places his inside hand down.

BLOCKING/PROGRESSION

There is only one basic block taught in the Wing-T, the shoulder block. As a result, the ends use the same blocking progression as the offensive lineman, which is described in Chapter 10. The only addition is that as the ends often have to run to a point before executing a block, the dummy is placed five yards away from the blocker in the final stage of the progression. The ends therefore have one additional step that they must run to the target being sure to get their feet into the proper position as they make their approach.

BLOCKING TECHNIQUES

The tight end must master exactly the same blocks described in Chapter 10 for the offensive lineman. The split end, however, because he is lined up away from the formations, must learn two additional blocks:

1. *Crack Block:* The crack block is used to establish the flank when running a play to the split end side. The wide position of the split end places him at an advantage in that he has an outside angle both on the strong safety and on any linebacker to the inside. When executing the crack block, the split end will release upfield for two steps and then break to the inside looking for the strong safety or a linebacker. His angle must be sharp enough to prevent penetration. To complete the block he should place his head to the inside and make contact above the waist (Figure 11-1).

2. *Stalk Block:* The stalk block is used by split ends, tight ends, and halfbacks to control the defensive back responsible for covering the deep third in the secondary. The offensive player will release off the line of scrimmage simulating a deep pass pattern. Once the cushion between the offensive and defensive players is reduced to three yards, as the defensive player stops retreating, the offensive player will come under control, square his feet, and mirror the defensive player, making

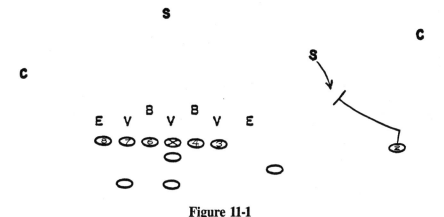

Figure 11-1

sure that he keeps himself between the running back and the defensive player. He must never let the defensive player get past him to the inside (Figure 11-2).

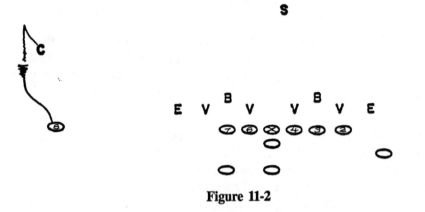

Figure 11-2

RELEASES

There are three basic releases used by the tight end and the split end to avoid being held up at the line of scrimmage by a defensive player aligned head up on them. These three releases are:

1. *Grass Out Release:* This release is used primarily by the tight end to get into the secondary quickly to run a pass pattern or to go to the cutoff. In order to execute the grass out release the tight end fires out, fully extending his body so that he is on all fours. He must be extremely low as he fires out in order to get under the defensive player. This initial move can be to the inside or to the outside depending on the play being run. Once he gets to an even up position with the defensive player, he should push off his hands to recover to two points and get into his pattern (Figure 11-3).

2. *Head and Shoulder Fake Release:* This release is used by both the tight end and the split end, but more often by the split end because of all the room he has to operate. As the name implies, the receiver simply fakes releasing one way and quickly releases the other way. For example, if an outside release is preferred, the receiver steps inside with his inside foot, faking in that direction with both his head and shoulders. He then pushes off the inside foot and sprints to the outside, getting into the pattern. As with the grass out release, he must be low in order to get under the defensive player (Figure 11-4).

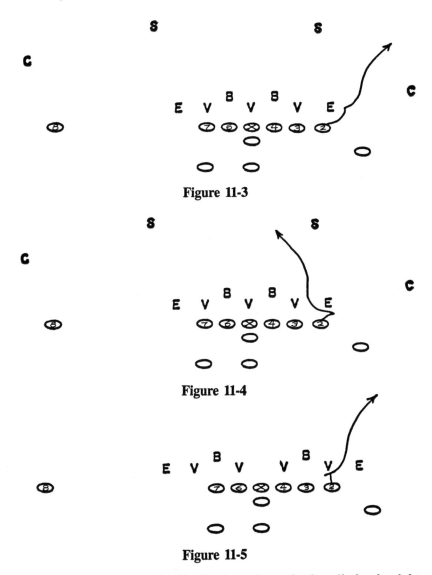

Figure 11-3

Figure 11-4

Figure 11-5

3. *Block Release:* The block release is used primarily by the tight end, but can be used by the split end as well. In executing the block release, the receiver explodes into the defensive player, using his shoulder block technique. His head should be placed to the side to which he wants to release, that is, to the outside for an outside release. After exploding into the defensive player, he should disengage quickly and release into his pattern. As with the other releases, he must be low in order to get under the defensive player (Figure 11-5).

PASS PATTERNS

There are a variety of pass routes that the split end and tight end may run as indicated by the route tree used in the Wing-T system (Figure 11-6). There are, however, only five general areas into which a pattern may be run. The five general areas and the primary routes for both the split end and the tight end in each area are listed below.

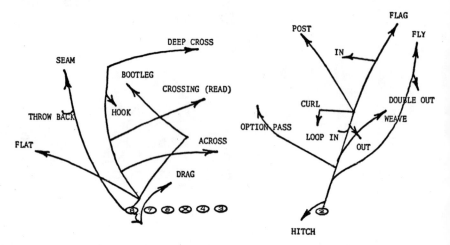

Figure 11-6

A. Short Outside;
   1. Split End; Out (Weave)
   2. Tight End; Seam
B. Short Inside;
   1. Split End; Curl
   2. Tight End; Hook
C. Deep Outside;
   1. Split End; Fly
   2. Tight End; Waggle
D. Deep Inside;
   1. Split End; Post
   2. Tight End; Deep Cross
E. Quick Inside;
   1. Split End; Slant or Option Pass
   2. Tight End; Cross

A. Short Outside:
 1. Split End; Out (Weave);
  a. vs. Three-Deep Zone

   Release with quick width to get on the outside shoulder of 5. (Refer to Chapter 4 for a description of the numbering of defensive personnel.) The depth of the pattern will vary from eight yards to twelve yards, depending on the backfield action.

   While this depth will vary, it is imperative that the cut be made back to the line of scrimmage. If the ball is not thrown by the second step after the cut, loop in and adjust to the quarterback (Figure 11-7).

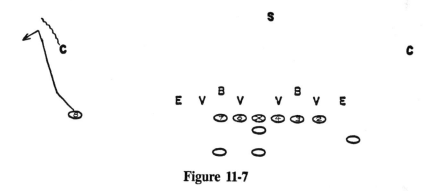

Figure 11-7

  b. vs. Two-Deep Zone (Weave)

   Release with quick width. As 5 rolls up to become 4, avoid contact by adjusting to the inside. Weave back to the outside and adjust to the open area. The depth will be determined by the backfield action and the amount of delay that 4 causes in the release (Figure 11-8).

  c. vs. Man

   Release through the defensive back's inside shoulder. Continue to create inside pressure until the breaking point is reached. Once again, the depth of the breaking will be determined by the backfield

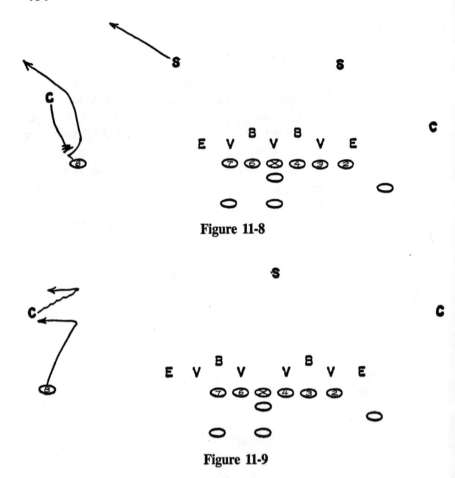

Figure 11-8

Figure 11-9

action. Cut sharply to the outside and run away from the defensive back (Figure 11-9).

2. Tight End; Seam
   a. vs. Three-Deep Zone or Two-Deep Zone;

   Release outside for a point seven yards deep and three yards outside. Read the cornerback and react accordingly. If the corner rolls up to cover the flat, adjust the pattern into the seam created between the corner and the safety. If the corner stays deep, adjust through his outside shoulder. The ball should be caught over the outside shoulder (Figure 11-10).

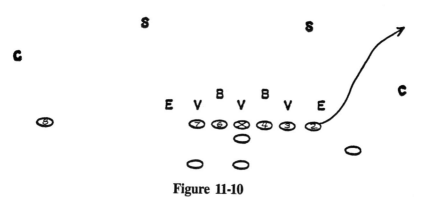

Figure 11-10

b. vs. Man;

Release outside and quickly work directly upfield. Create inside pressure on the defensive back by adjusting the pattern through his inside shoulder. When a depth of seven yards is reached, bend to the outside and run away from the coverage (Figure 11-11).

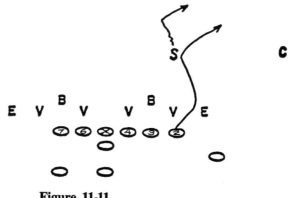

Figure 11-11

B. Short Inside
   1. Split End; Curl;
      a. vs. Three-Deep Zone or Man;

         Release with quick width to get on the outside shoulder of 5, then work directly upfield. Stop at a depth of fourteen yards and turn sharply back to the inside. Locate the linebackers as you turn in and adjust accordingly (Figure 11-12).

b. vs. Two-Deep Zone;

Release with quick width. As 5 rolls up to become 4, avoid contact by adjusting quickly to the inside. Return to the original path and execute the cut (Figure 11-13).

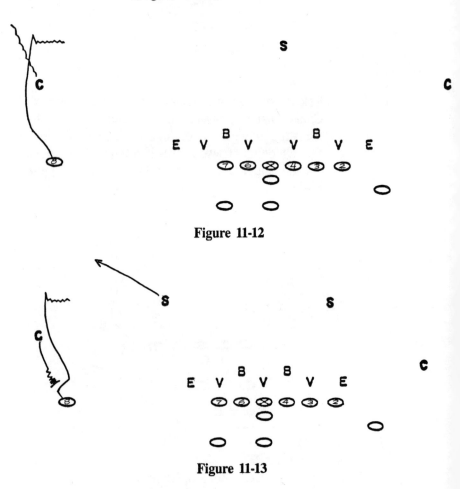

Figure 11-12

Figure 11-13

2. Tight End; Hook

a. vs. All Coverage;

Release outside and work upfield to a depth of twelve yards. Turn sharply back to the inside and adjust to the open area away from the linebackers (Figure 11-14).

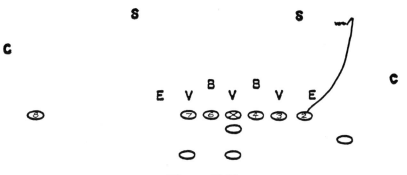

Figure 11-14

C. Deep Outside
   1. Split End; Fly;
      a. vs. All Coverage;

      Release with quick width simulating an out cut. At the point where the out cut would occur, bend to the outside and accelerate upfield. Catch the ball over the inside shoulder (Figure 11-15).

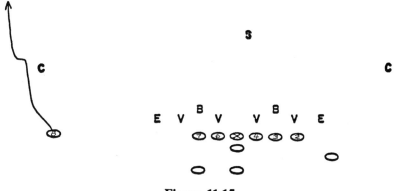

Figure 11-15

   2. Tight End; Waggle;
      a. vs. All Coverage;

      Step inside with the inside foot, simulating a down block. Stay low to avoid being held up and accelerate to the flag. Catch the ball over the outside shoulder. If a defensive player is lined up in the gap, make contact with the inside shoulder before releasing (Figure 11-16).

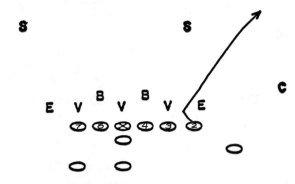

Figure 11-16

D. Deep Inside;
  1. Split End; Post;
    a. vs. All Coverage;
      Release with quick width, simulating a fly pattern. At a depth of twelve yards, fake to the outside and cut sharply for the near post (Figure 11-17).

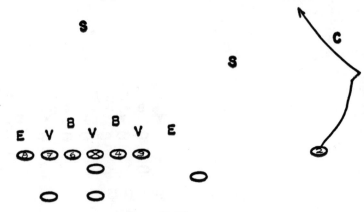

Figure 11-17

  2. Tight End; Deep Cross;
    a. vs. Three-Deep Zone;
      Release inside and get to a depth of five yards to clear the linebackers. Cross through the middle of

the secondary and read the safety. If the safety stays in the middle, continue across and turn upfield between the safety and the far cornerback (Figure 11-18).

b. vs. Two-Deep Zone;

The release is the same as it is against three deep. In reading the safety, adjust deep through the middle as he (the safety) takes off to cover deep outside (Figure 11-19).

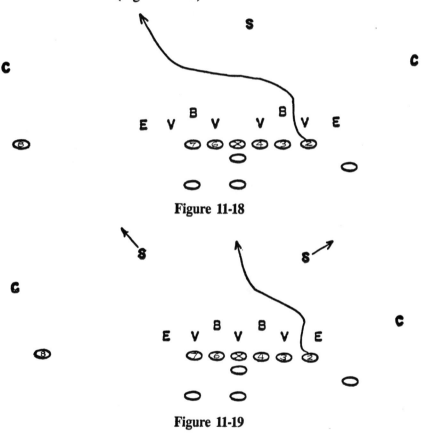

Figure 11-18

Figure 11-19

E. Quick Inside:
1. Split End; Slant (Option Pass)
   a. vs. Three-Deep Zone;

   Release upfield for two steps, then break sharply into the middle. Read 4 and adjust path accordingly.

As 4 steps up to play the pitch, bend path behind him and work directly upfield (Figure 11-20).

b. vs. Two-Deep Zone;

Avoid contact on the release as 4 rolls up. Read the safety (5) to determine when to bend upfield. It is important not to get too far inside before bending the pattern upfield in order to avoid getting hit by the linebacker (Figure 11-21).

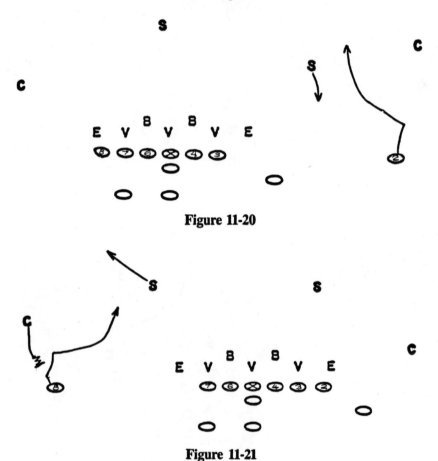

Figure 11-20

Figure 11-21

2. Tight End; Cross;
    a. vs. All Coverage;

Release inside and adjust depth to avoid the near side linebacker. Go in front of him or behind him depending on his depth. Adjust the speed of the pattern to avoid being covered by the far linebacker. Settle into the open area. The depth should be between eight and twelve yards (Figure 11-22).

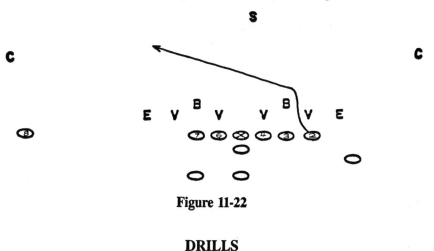

Figure 11-22

DRILLS

The drills used for receivers are designed to improve cutting ability and catching ability.

1. Cutting Drill:

    The best cutting drill is set up by placing four cones in an area ten yards long and ten yards wide. This forces the receivers to make four forty-five degree cuts, two off of each foot. This drill starts at a slow pace and the speed increases as the players' proficiency increases (Figure 11-23).

2. Catching Drill:

    The receivers face each other at a distance of five yards and throw the ball sharply to each other. The emphasis of this drill is to keep the eyes on the ball. The ball should be thrown at the numbers, over the head, and at either knee.

3. Fly Drill:

    This drill is used as a continuation of the warmup period, as well as a drill to run under the ball and catch it. The receivers line up ten yards away from the quarterback on the right side (on alternate days, line up on the left side) and run down field on the quarterback's command. The ball is thrown over the

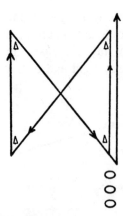

Figure 11-23

outside shoulder with a trajectory that enables the receiver to adjust to the ball. After catching the ball, the receiver continues downfield for a reasonable distance and gives the ball to another quarterback and lines up to the right of this quarterback. He then heads back to the original quarterback when it is his turn. As the receivers and quarterbacks get loose, the receivers should widen to fifteen yards and the quarterbacks should increase their distance from each other (Figure 11-24).

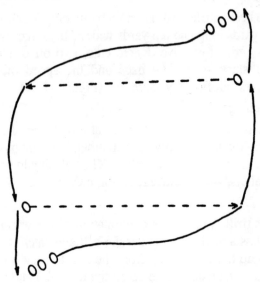

Figure 11-24

4. Comeback Drill:

The receiver lines up fifteen yards from the coach and runs directly at the coach. The coach throws the ball sharply at him. This forces the receiver to catch the ball away from his body with soft hands (Figure 11-25).

5. Bad Ball Drill:

The receiver lines up on a particular yard line and the coach lines up ten yards away. The receiver runs down the line and catches balls thrown low and away by the coach. This drill forces the receiver to get his hands under the ball and cradle it into his body as he rolls (Figure 11-26).

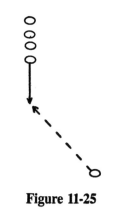

Figure 11-25

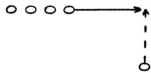

Figure 11-26

6. Gauntlet Drill:

The receiver runs a forty-five degree pattern to catch the ball over his outside shoulder. As soon as he catches the ball, he turns upfield and runs through a gauntlet. This forces him to put the ball away quickly (Figure 11-27).

7. Sideline Drill:

The receiver lines up five yards inside the sideline and releases with width. He makes his cut at eight yards. The coach throws

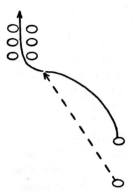

Figure 11-27

the ball at the sideline forcing the receiver to catch the ball and concentrate on having one foot touch inbounds (Figure 11-28).

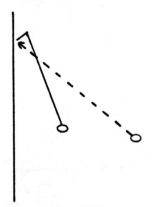

Figure 11-28

See Chapter 8 for combination drills with the quarterbacks.

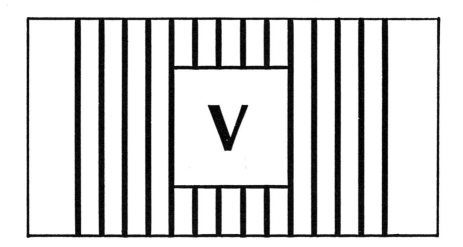

ORGANIZATION FOR SUCCESS

12

THE TEACHING PROGRESSION

Your practice organization should reflect the major thing you ask of your athletes—a drive for perfection. Developing an organization for success is your way of showing the importance of practice and your interest in assisting them.

The development of practice plans begins by listing all the things you want your team to know for the first game and then the schedule. The next step is to structure objectives for blocks of days, i.e., we would like to be prepared for a controlled scrimmage on the fifth practice using these plays. We will need some recovery time to progress to a more sophisticated scrimmage that might include situations and then select a date for a final game-type scrimmage, in preparation for the first game.

Once you know what material your team will need, and have assigned objectives for blocks of days, you are ready to set up objectives for each day that will lead to those block objectives. We feel that our teams can digest about four offensive plays each day for the first few days and then two or three new plays in addition to two or three that are phases of plays that have been introduced after that. Provision should also be made for the defense or defenses you would like to run against each day.

Following is an example of a recent preseason teaching progression for offense. Some consideration is always given to the defense when designing this progression as we will have to demonstrate for each other early. Note the reason we begin with the spread formation is because our defensive teaching lends itself to starting with the spread.

UNIVERSITY OF DELAWARE PRESEASON
PRACTICE OBJECTIVES AND TEACHING PROGRESSION

<u>MONDAY - AUGUST 20</u>

8:00 - 8:15	WELCOME-CAMP ROUTINE, DAY'S OBJECTIVES DISTRIBUTE KEYS - ROOM ASSIGNMENTS
8:30 - 12:15	PHYSICALS BY GROUP

<u>OFFENSIVE ORIENTATION</u>

<u>INTRODUCE OFFENSE VS. 55</u>

1. WHY WING-T PHILO?	1. SPR 121 T. OPT, PASS
2. NUMBERING SYSTEM	2. SPR 124 ON
3. HUDDLE - CADENCE PROCEDURE	3. SPR 121 WAG
4. TAKEOFF	4. SPR 187
5. SPR 100 - BLUE FORMATIONS	5. PATTERNS: POST, FLY, UP, CURL, OUT 8, 12 YD. (DOUBLE OUT)

11:45 - 12:30

<u>DEFENSIVE ORIENTATION</u>

<u>12:30 - 1:15 LUNCH (PRESS INTRO & WELCOME)</u>

1:30 - 1:45	GROUP PROCESSING
2:00 - 4:00	CHECK EQUIPMENT — PICTURE PERIOD
4:00 - 6:00	PHYSICAL TESTING
6:45 - 7:30	DINNER
7:30 - 8:00	TEAM MEETING - KICKING GAME ORIENTATION

<u>1. TUESDAY—AUGUST 21</u> (FIRST NONCONTACT)
TEACHING—ORIENTATION
INTRO P.A.T. & FIELD GOAL

<u>INTRODUCE OFFENSE VS. 55</u>

1. SPR 134 CT.
2. SPR 199 OPT.
3. BLUE 23 G.T.
4. SPR 159 SEAM
5. BLUE 59 SEAM
6. GOAL LINE PATTERN POINTS

2. WEDNESDAY—AUGUST 22 (SECOND NONCONTACT)
INTRODUCE OFFENSE VS. 55 THEN 40

1. 121, RED 21
2. SPR 134 CT SHORT
3. 187 XB
4. 199 OPT
5. 159 OUT
6. 129 TRAP OPT
7. "JUMP TO"
   "SHIFT TO"
8. "SLIDE TO"

3. THURSDAY—AUGUST 23 (THIRD NONCONTACT)
INTRODUCE OFFENSE VS. 55 THEN 40

1. 131, RED 31
2. 134 CT B/L
3. 189 OPT
4. SPR 181 K.P. C & FLY
5. BLUE 51 C & O, C & FLY
6. RED 29 WAG T.E. HOOK
7. RED 21 WAG OUT, CURL

4. FRIDAY—AUGUST 24 (FIRST CONTACT)
                    ONE ON ONE—SHOULDER SHOTS
                    PASS PRO & PASS RUSH
INTRODUCE OFFENSE VS. WT 60

1. BLUE 124, 124 LH
2. 132
3. SPR 134 CT AT 8
4. BLUE 31 OPT WALL
5. RED 82 DOWN, Z
6. 199 OPT. PASS
7. 129
8. 129 B/L

5. SATURDAY— AUGUST 25 (INTRO MIXED GROUP WORK)
                    INTRO SCRIMMAGE—800 FILMED SCRIMMAGE
INTRODUCE OFFENSE VS. GAPS (41-49)

1. 189 KP
2. 189 OPT (L)

3. RED 82 DOWN OPT
4. BLUE 53 DRAW
5. RED 59 SC T.E. RT
6. BLUE 51 TH BK
7. T 983 ON
8. T 991 OPT (L)
9. T 944 WEDGE
10. "PORT TO"—"STAR TO"
11. RT, LT.

6. SUNDAY— AUGUST 26 (NO CONTACT—RECOVER FROM
        SCRIMMAGE)
        NO A.M. MEETING—CHURCH
INTRODUCE OFFENSE VS. 55 (52-58)

1. BLUE 21 CT XX AT NINE
2. 189 WAG
3. RED 61 JET
4. 169 CURL
5. I 132, I 133 ON
6. *BLUE 51 C & O & HOOK

7. MONDAY— AUGUST 27 CONTROLLING CLOCK—
        HURRY, ON THE BALL
        OFFENSE—REVIEW DAY—DEFENSIVE HURRY
        PROCEDURES
INTRODUCE OFFENSE VS. 55
DOUBLE SET "SCRAMBLE TO"
DOUBLE SET "RUN AWAY" BLUE
NO MO 189 WAG
181 WAG IN

8. TUESDAY— AUGUST 28 800 FILMED SCRIMMAGE
        (SITUATION ORIENTED)
INTRODUCE OFFENSE VS. 345 STACK

1. 126 G.T., GUT VS 40 ON VS 55
2. SPR NO MO 187 WHAM
3. BLUE 34 CT
4. RT 122 GUT
5. RED 61 RH DRAG, RH AT 5

9. WEDNESDAY— AUGUST 29 (RECOVER FROM SCRIMMAGE— NO CONTACT)

INTRODUCE OFFENSE VS. 40, 55

SHORT LIST REVIEW

1. *BLUE 51 HITCH RH (QUICK SCREEN)
2. BLUE 38 CT XX (SPR 138 CT XX)
3. SPR NO MO 189 PITCH

10. THURSDAY— AUGUST 30 (TEAM PICTURE— PREP FOR SCRIMMAGE)

SHORT LIST REVIEW
INTRODUCE OFFENSE VS. 40 OFF

1. T 181 KP OPP
2. *RED 51, TE OUT
3. SPR 181 KP F.B. OPP
4. RED NO MO 29 WAG BK, SWITCH

11. FRIDAY—AUGUST 31 (FINAL SCRIMMAGE)

1 & 2 VS. LOWER LEVEL

                                    DEMO VS. 1 THEN 2

12. SATURDAY—SEPTEMBER 1   A.M. WALK THRU
                    PLAYERS LEAVE FOLLOWING PRACTICE

13. SUNDAY—SEPTEMBER 2   PLAYERS RETURN 5:00 P.M.
                    REVIEW SPECIAL TEAM ASSIGNMENTS

14. MONDAY—SEPTEMBER 3   JAMES MADISON WEEK

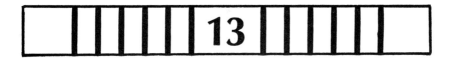

PERFECT PRACTICE
MAKES PERFECT

There seem to be a number of misconceptions about football practice that you should clarify with your team from the beginning. First, contrary to the old addage, "practice makes perfect," I read recently that only perfect practice makes perfect. We believe this at Delaware and all of us, players and coaches alike, recognize that we probably won't play a bit better in a game than we have practiced during the week.

Second, I have noticed there is a feeling among many players that they will suddenly have the intensity necessary to win when they play in the game. It is our opinion that a team develops speed and intensity levels during practice that will determine their game hardness and the quality of their play. Practicing at half speed would be analagous to a baseball player taking batting practice against a pitcher throwing underhand. It wouldn't help him prepare for a game. We're going to insist that our team's practice be game quality!

Practice at Delaware begins with our players warming up with stretching, followed by a series of running skills. Then each group is coached in "shoulder skills," while the quarterbacks receive snaps from the centers. Group work continues with each coach teaching individual skills that will be needed to fulfill the day's objectives during team work.

It should be mentioned that our backfield technique is taught and drilled first with the quarterback executing his footwork without a ball carrier. Then we will move into handoff drills where the quarterback will hand the ball off to a back with a specific technique, and finally run it with a full backfield to develop the faking necessary for a successful play.

Group work is divided into two general categories; fundamentals and specific skills. Between these two we will run what we call "mixed agility." This is a continuous circuit drill with all players running through seven stations. During this drill all coaches will have an opportunity to observe all of the players each day, but the real value of "mixed agility" is conditioning and forced recovery in the middle of practice because this drill is always followed by an instruction period.

Following group work, we will practice in units involving players from two or more groups. We refer to this as "mixed group" work. This practice period is designed to give all of our players the feeling that "I've been here before" when they get into the game and is skeletal in nature.

The final phase of our practice is team work, which is sometimes followed by wind sprints or gassers. We run them everyday in preseason practice for about 11 days, then only on Tuesday during the season. I have heard that more games are lost on Wednesday or Thursday than on Saturday. I am certain this statement was made with respect to freshness, which is of primary importance to successful play, and we are careful about running our players too much.

Like preseason organization, each day of the week has its particular objectives.

Sunday

Game films are shown and corrections are made. Both the training room and weight room are available for treatment or lifting. No mention of our upcoming opponent is discussed.

Monday

Monday's practice design includes a lot of running, review of the kicking game and an introduction to our next opponent in a detailed scouting report. Players who did not play on Saturday will have a scrimmage opportunity and all will be introduced to a general plan of attack against our next opponent's basic defense.

Tuesday

Tuesday is our big day. It's the only day during the week that we scrimmage during the season, and it is the only day that we run gassers or wind sprints. Our work is directed to developing a game plan against the basic defensive philosophy of our upcoming opponent. Each team will scrimmage ten minutes, but prior to that they will practice at least ten minutes in "mixed group" work live. We feel that they will be able to take part in this drill with a limited risk of a real scrimmage situation. All the plays that we are going to use during the practice are listed so that we won't miss anything.

Wednesday

The objectives of Wednesday are similar to Tuesday, with the exception that the only live work that will be done will be "mixed group" work. We'll expand the game plan taking situations into consideration, i.e., what defenses do our opponents use in long yardage. Wednesday will include a substantial passing game against the long yardage defenses of our opponents. Wednesday is also the day that our quarterbacks receive the game plan so that they will know exactly what we are going to do and how we are going to attack a specific defense.

Thursday

Thursday is a total review day. It is a day with a lot of running, scheduled, but in reality it is a plan of rehersal. All of the offense to be used in the game will be practiced. Special emphasis is given to critical plays including short yardage and goal line. In addition we will run our opening sequence.

Friday

Friday is a review day with very little running, most of the time is spent in meetings.

ACTUAL PRACTICE SCHEDULE

MONDAY, OCTOBER 15
OBJECTIVES: INTRO GAME PLAN, RUN KICKING GAME,
    SCOUTING REPORT

UNIVERSITY OF DELAWARE VS. TEMPLE

3:30–4:05   MONDAY NIGHT LEAGUE
4:05–4:20   TEMPLE PICTURE & APP.
    4:20–4:40   GROUPWORK
        REV. 20 BLOCKING

4:40–4:50   <u>KICKING GAME RUNNING</u>
                   PUNT FROM 35 "OUT OF BOUNDS"

4:50–5:10   <u>SEVEN ON SEVEN (PLAYS)</u>
          SPR 181 KP SW & POST   BL 151
          *BL 51 <OUT, FLY, FLAT   RED 29 DEL. WAG.
          SPR 151 SCR LH LT–(RT.MID)   *RED 59 HIT. LH LT
          PRO BL 89–LO 189 KP SW. D.O.
          LO 929 WAG. CURL PRO BL 21 WAG. TE HOOK

5:10–5:30   <u>DIVIDED TEAMS</u>

          187 XB OPT   134 CT.   PRO RED 82 DO
          189 OPT   136 CT.   PRO RED 82 DO OPT
          129   126 GUT   123 G.T. LH
          121   LO 181 OPT   137 CT
          181 OPT   LO 183 GUT REL   137 CT XX
                       134 CT AT 8

5:30–5:40   <u>SIGNALS</u>
                   2 MIN. DRILL

TUESDAY, OCTOBER 16
OBJECTIVES: 10' PER GROUP LIVE MIXED 10' PER GROUP =
            SCRIMMAGE PLUS BASIC GAME PLAN, RUN
            GASSERS:

            UNIVERSITY OF DELAWARE VS. TEMPLE

3:30–4:05   <u>PASSING SITUATIONS</u>
   4:05–4:20   <u>GROUPWORK</u>

          136 CT.   183 GUT. REL.
          137 CT XX   PRO RED 82 DO.
                   981 OPT. VS. SECONDARY

4:20–4:35   <u>SEVEN ON SEVEN</u>   <u>345 STACK</u>

     *BL 51 <OUT, FLY, FLAT   BL 51
     181 KP   *BL 21 DEL WAG
     SL RED 81 KP   PRO BL 21 DEL. TE. HOOK
     LO 121 WAG. CURL   LO 151 SCR RH LT (RT MID)

4:35–4:55   <u>MIXED GROUPS</u>
     <u>FLANK</u>   <u>INTERNAL</u>

189 OPT *199 OPT (L)   134 CT AT 8   126 GUT
129   BL 81 OPT   136 CT   187 XB
X SPR 199 OPT (LH)   X SPR 187 XB (LH)

4:55–5:10   <u>PASSING GAME</u>
              <u>NORMAL</u>

RED 159 P.F.F.   SL RED 81 KP   929 WAG OUT
LO 151 SC LH LT   *SP 991 OPT (L)   989 HIT. RH FL
       MAN 245 ST
*RED 59 <O.F.F.
*RED 29 DEL. WAG

5:10–5:20   <u>KICKING GAME</u>
5:20–5:40   <u>DIVIDED TEAMS</u>   <u>345 ST.</u>
   936 CT B/L   933 CT XX   934 CT
   129   BL 24 GUT   LO 187 XB
   983 XB   LO 136 CT   LO 921

WEDNESDAY, OCTOBER 17
OBJECTIVES: SIT. PASSING, GAME PLAN MEETING (QB)

UNIVERSITY OF DELAWARE VS. TEMPLE

3:15–3:50   (3:30)   <u>GROUP MEETINGS</u>
   3:55–4:25   <u>GROUPWORK</u>
   136 CT   SPR 983 XB
   RED 37 CT   PRO RED 82 DO
   LO 981 OPT   PRO RED 82 DO. OPT

4:25–4:40   <u>SEVEN ON SEVEN</u>   <u>MAN 200</u>

SL 181 KP   SPR 181 KP SW   *BL 51 <O.F.F.
PRO RED 81 KP   *BL 51 <O.F.F.   SPR 181 KP WG. OUT

4:55–5:15   <u>PASSING GAME</u>

SPR 159 S.F.F.   SP 936 CT B/L   SPR 151 SC LH LT
  PRO RED 51 HK.   989 KP (CHG)   BL 51
RED 29 WAG (CHG) RED 59   SP 181 KP

MAN 345 ST & DR (FR)
SL 181 KP
929 WAG CURL
PRO BL 89 KP

5:15–5:25	TEAMWORK	
SPR 187 XB	RED 37 CT	LO 134 CT - 8
*SP 991 OPT(L)	SP 134 CT B/L	BL 33 CT
936 CT AT 2	SL 134 CT B/L	BL 83 CT
BL 29 (CHG)	RED 89 OPT	RED 26 GUT
SPR 983 XB	PRO RED 82 DO OPT X SPR 187 SX (LH)	

KICKING SPECIALTIES

THURSDAY, OCTOBER 17
OBJECTIVES: REVIEW - POLISH (OPENING SEQUENCE)

UNIVERSITY OF DELAWARE VS. TEMPLE

3:30–3:50	GROUP MEETING	
3:55–4:20	GROUP WORK	
4:20–4:30	SY & G.L.	PAT

*SPR 991 OPT		
(GL)	SPR 187 ON	*121 WAG TH BK
FL I 137 ON	181 KP	PRO RED FB MOT
		QB DRAW

4:30–4:55	PASSING GAME	NORMAL
SP 981 KP	PRO RED FB MOT	
	QB DRAW	*BL51 HIT
LO 189 KP	BL 59	*RED 59 <O.F.F.
LO 921 WAG	RED 83 GUT REL	*BL 51 P.F.F.
PRO BL 89 KP	PRO RED 81 KP	
*BL 53 DR		

4:55–5:10   KICKING GAME

1. K.O.
2. 3RD DOWN
3. DEF OF KICKING

5:10–5:35   <u>DIVIDED TEAMS (1 & 2 DUMMIES)</u>

X SPR 983 XB RH	SPR 187 XB	BL 29
134 CT B/L	SPR 983 XB	181 HITCH FLARE
BL 88 DO OPT		989 HIT RH
		FLARE
X SPR 187 XB LH	934 CT	X SPR 199 OPT

THE VARIABLES OF OFFENSIVE FOOTBALL

There are many variables in offensive football over which you have direct control—the formation you call on, the type of play, and so forth. But there are several variables over which you have no control that must be taken into consideration as you select a play.

The variables of a football game in order of their importance are:

1. score
2. time
3. field position (vertical)
4. down and distance
5. wind and weather
6. personnel
7. game plan
8. defense opposing you

Score

The score of the game is a variable that does not change rapidly. You will have plenty of time to regard the score, and it will affect your selection of plays with respect to the degree of conservativeness that you will display. It is commonly regarded as a sound procedure to play conservatively when ahead by eight points. You may loosen up again when you are more than eight points ahead. Regard a one to six point lead as slightly better than a tie, but you need to score again. Take some chances when you are behind but these chances should be related to the time remaining in the game, how many points you are behind, and your vertical field position. You may take reasonable chances when the score is tied, but remember, *a tie is better than a loss.*

Summarizing, with eight points ahead, let your opponents make mistakes. With one to six points up, you need another score.

Time

Time is the most predictable variable and you may use its consistency to your advantage. This variable affects your decisions most near half time or at the end of the game, giving rise to the popular term "two minute offense."

You will always find yourself in one of two situations regarding playing time: you need to conserve time or you need to consume time.

When you are conserving time you would like the clock stopped after each down and not started until you snap the ball for the next play. You may create this time-conserving situation by stopping the clock in the following ways:

1. calling a time out (you have three per half and none should be used for anything but conserving time)
2. an incomplete pass
3. a ball carrier going out of bounds
4. when you first receive possession of the ball
5. to complete a penalty for an infraction by the defensive teams with less then twenty-five seconds remaining in the second and fourth quarters.

Recognize that the clock starts at two times when your team is on offense.

1. when the referee spots the ball and signals it ready for play
2. when the ball is snapped

The first incident expends time as the clock is running while your team is in the huddle. The latter conserves playing time as the clock will not start until the ball is snapped.

If there is limited time remaining and you are forced into a time-conserving situation, make sure that you know the number of time outs remaining. Remind your backs to get out of bounds with a live ball. Get the clock stopped as quickly as possible using one of these methods, after which the clock is started on the snap. Work toward the sidelines, but if you take a shot at a crossing pattern, be ready to follow it with a time out or "on the ball." Don't panic, we moved the ball 90 yards in 47 seconds in the 1968 Boardwalk Bowl. It doesn't have to be done in one play. Use automatics at the line when time outs are gone.

When consuming time, keep the ball in play and avoid a penalty call. Know how many time outs your opponents have remaining because they will force the clock to start with the snap as often as possible. Use sweeps to consume time, and in certain situations it is wise to give ground. Use the quarterback sneak, but instruct your quarterback to get his knee to the ground before contact as you cannot lose possession if the ball is dead. This is also the method for taking a safety if the score permits and we do not want to kick out of the end zone.

Field Position

The field is divided into five vertical zones, each of which demand certain consideration (Figure 14-1).

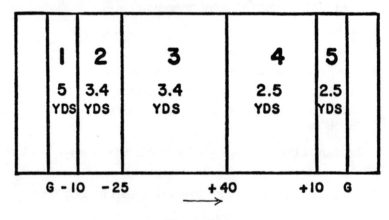

Figure 14-1

You should think in terms of controlling the ball by making the necessary yardage. Generally the requirement of each down is 3.4 yards as you must consider kicking on the fourth down if you are not successful in gaining ten yards in three tries. However, there are certain zones that suggest kicking on third down and some in which it would be foolish to kick. These factors give the zone different down requirements.

ZONE 1 (Your goal line to your ten-yard line)

1. *Your yardage requirement per down is five yards* because you must consider kicking on third down when your kicker must kick near the out-of-bounds line. Get your kicker enough room!
2. Consider wedge and sneak first. Do not attempt to run outside, but you may run 4 CT. - 6 CT. if you are near the five-yard line.
3. If you are faced with a strong wind with thirty seconds or less, use time so that you will be able to kick with the wind in the next quarter.
4. Kick on first down if the quarter change will give you a strong wind disadvantage.
5. If you can execute an action pass without throwing from your own end zone, you may be able to get out of the hole. Throw the ball out of bounds if the receiver is covered.

ZONE 2 (from your ten-yard line to your twenty-five)

1. Your yardage requirement per down is 3.4 yards as you no longer need to consider kicking on the third down.
2. Use some discretion when throwing, i.e., avoid passes that are thrown in the middle.

ZONE 3 (from your twenty-five to your opponent's forty)

1. Your yardage requirement per down is still 3.4 yards.
2. Use normal game plan.
3. When nearing Zone 4, you will receive assistance with the decision to punt on fourth down or not.

ZONE 4 (from your opponent's forty to their ten)

1. Your yardage requirement per down is now 2.5 yards and you may forget about kicking.
2. Scoring may be easier from this Zone than Zone 5; put your best plays together now!
3. Third and four or five yards to go is no longer a passing situation while second and one or two yards to go suggests passing for the touchdown as you, in all probability, can pick up the first down on the third and fourth try.

4. As you near the fifteen-yard line, and if you are running out of downs, be aware of gaining field position for a field goal attempt.

ZONE 5 (from your opponent's ten to their goal line)
1. Use regular offense—do not consider you are in goal line situation unless you are inside the four-yard line.
2. When the down requirement becomes one yard or less, i.e., first and goal on the four-yard line or less, use direct shots inside. Don't risk the loss of yardage.
3. Outside game may be your best opportunity, use regular one and nine plays.
4. 34 CT. - 36 CT. are still good plays.
5. Do not throw pattern passes.

Down and Distance

It is not difficult to be alert to the variables of score, wind, weather, personnel, and game plan. They tend to change slowly in comparison to field position, down, and distance to go. Always get a graphical picture of down and distance by looking for the sideline stakes and repeating the situation to yourself; "I have three downs to make four yards."

You must continually be aware of the zone you are in so that you can determine the down requirement of each play. If you divide the yards to go by the number of downs available, you will provide yourself with the necessary information to prevent the bad call. If the answer turns out to be less than four, you should consider running the ball. If the answer becomes four or more, consider throwing the ball. If the answer comes out to less than one, use the down to set something else up or go for the score; this is called a "purpose down." Remember, there is no one perfect selection, but many times there is one bad call. *This is the one to avoid.*

Down Requirements and Suggested Calls

1. First and ten (in 3.5 Zone) Suggests a running play as the down requirement is 3.5 or less than four. Remember, however, that you have several passes that are considered to be in the running category. Passes usually have a higher percentage of completion on early downs.

2. First and ten (in 2.5 Zone) Suggests grind out type of offense. An incomplete pass early makes your down requirement 3.5 again.

3. The division rule will guide you where you have more than one down for a given amount of yardage. This difficult decision involves situations in which you have a single down to pick up a given amount of yardage. The following are suggested for the listed particular situations:

   a. One down remaining to pick up three to four yards. You should make this situation 75 percent of the time. Use the ground play that has been going—running outside to a spread end after you have thrown to him would be sound. Passes that threaten the flank are excellent in this situation as they present you with the option of run or pass. The exact demands of the play will influence your execution; i.e., if you have a three-yard requirement—don't look for the long aspect of any pass—*get the required yardage.*

   b. One down remaining to pick up five to seven yards. You should be able to make this 50 percent of the time. This situation requires that you execute perfectly. Hit sideline or man in the flat. Screen or draw type plays may be effective.

   c. One down remaining to pick up more than eight yards. Defenses are generally as situation conscious as you are and will anticipate long drop-back passes, ignoring the threat of run imposed by action passes. This fact should be used in your selection of a play in long yardage situation. Screen and draw are excellent considerations if the down requirement is more than eight yards, but because the secondary is oriented deep, it is often effective to hit crossing end as the intermediate zones are not only difficult to cover, but open further by the retreat of the deep defenders. Moving the ball to the flanks often evades the pressure of aggressive rush by ends. They may be even so pass conscious that 4 CT. - 6 CT. might do the job for you.

Wind and Weather

Nature's effect on the game is highly overrated and it is usually a good idea to make no changes in your plan until you are actually on the field. Rain may enhance your passing game as it is easier for your receivers to run forward than it is for the defenders to run backwards. Wind probably affects the game more than any other natural factor. Use a strong wind to your advantage in kicking on a windy day. If you have only a few seconds to go in the first or third quarter with a strong wind at your back, it may be wise to kick on an early down unless you are certain of a reasonable drive. Don't kick the ball into a gale for any reason.

Personnel

Study the abilities of your teammates and make use of their special abilities. Call on your hardest back for crucial situations. Throw to the receiver who will catch the ball. Don't be a politician—get the job done.

Game Plan (Fig. 14-2)

The game plan should be written by Wednesday. It should include plays that are described as either primary or secondary plays. The primary plays should be relatively few in number and should be used before secondary plays. Primary plays always appear in red on the game plan, but may be changed during the game. The game plan will give you a complete understanding of our attack plan and you will be relatively free to make your own selections during each drive.

DEFENSE OPPOSING YOU - (Has been described in Chapter 5)

GAME PLAN
UNIVERSITY OF DELAWARE VS. TEMPLE
OCTOBER 20, 1984

1. Temple uses a split 345 Stack Defensive. When coverage conscious their "stud" will change with their end. They have played some man, (with fire or drive) and have rolled to zone 200. Their alternate fronts are 40, (vs. double wing) and some free 255 in passing situations.

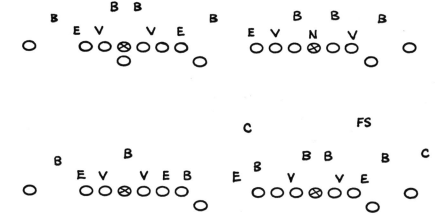

2. Your game plan begins as a controlled risk plan—relax and make it happen—execute. Mix formations, cadence, and situations.

3. Begin your running attack by forcing 3 to seal your tackle shoulder and stop your fullback:

RED, PRO 82 DO–BLUE PRO 88 DO   X SPR 187 XB LH–SPR 983 XB
LO 134 CT AT 8–LO 936 CT AT 2   RH

187 XB–983 SB
SPR 187 XB–SPR 983 XB

4. Now break contain for sweep, keep pass and option.
LO 129–LO 921   189 OPT–981 OPT (LO)
                             BLUE 81 OPT–RED 89 OPT
LO 121 WAG–LO 929 WAG, IND 134 CT B/L–936 CT B/L
189 KP–981 KP, SW & D.O.

5. Run at 4 and 6 with direct and counter action when backer's chase:

PRO, * RED 26 GUT–PRO,* BLUE 24 GUT
USE 4 CT–6 CT FROM ALL FORMATIONS.

6. Use XX CT, 33-37 CT, and gut release as passing to 3's contain.

7. Your passing game continues:

181 KP–989 KP   LO 134 CT B/L–LO 936 CT B/L
LQ 189 KP–LO 981 KP, SW DO   121 WAG–929 WAG
SPR 181 KP–SPR 989 KP, SW,DO   LO 129 WAG–LO 921 WAG, LED
LO 181 HIT–LO 989 HIT   *SPR 121 WAG SW–*SPR 929 WAG SW

159–951   PRO BL 21 DEL WAG-PRO RED 29 DEL WAG
*159–*951 IND
*SPR 159–*SPR 951 SEAM, FLY, FLAT
PRO BL 59 T.E. HOOK–PRO RED 51 T.E. HOOK
*BL 51–*RED 59, IND.

LO 151 SC LE LT–LO 951 SC RH RT
*BL 51 SC RH LT–*RED 59 SC LH RT

*SP 199 OPT (L)   181 OPT
129   137 CT XX   123 G.T. LH   121
189 OPT   187 XB   182 DO   182 DO OPT

O   O   O   O   O   O   O

O
SP 134 CT B/L   121 WAG, IND
159, OUT, CURL, L OUT   SP 136 CT B/L   129 WAG   181 KP
*59 IND   SP, 189 KP, SW & D.O.
O   O

                                                         LO 183
LO 187 x XB OPT   GUT REL LO 181 OPT
LO 129   LO 134 CT AT 8LO 136 CT LO 134 CT
LO 189 OPT
O   O   O   O   O   O   O

O
LO 129 WAG
LO 151 SC LH LT   LO 121 WAG, IND   LO 189 KP, SW & DO
O   O

LO 181 HIT LH FLARE

X SPR 187 XB LM
SPR 187 XB
/ X SPR 199 OPT LH SPR 134 CT AT 8   SPR 183 GUT REL   SPR 181 OPT

O   O   O   O   O   O   O
            O   O

*SPR 159 SEAM,FLY,FLAT   *SPR 121 WAG SW   SL 181 KP
                       X SPR 131 WAG   SPR 181 KP, SW *&DO
      O   O   CURL FLY
                                             POST FLY

PRO PL 33 DP OPT   PRO BL 88 DO
                      *BLUE 53 DRAW
BL 29   BL 88 DO
BL 83 DO OPT   BL 87 GUT NEL.   *BLUE 24 GUT   *BL 89 GUT REL   BL 81 OPT

      O   O   O   O   O   O   O
   O   O   O

                             PRO BLUE 21 DEL WAG TE HOOK
RED BL 59 T.E. HOOK   BLUE 29 WAG
                       O   / *BLUE 21 DBL WAG
BLUE 51, BLUE 59 SEAM AT 5
*BLUE 51 CURL, FLY, FLAT-POST, FLY, FLAT
                L CUT, FLY, FLAT   BLUE 81 KP, IND
 * BLUE 51 SC RH RT   PRO BL 89 KP

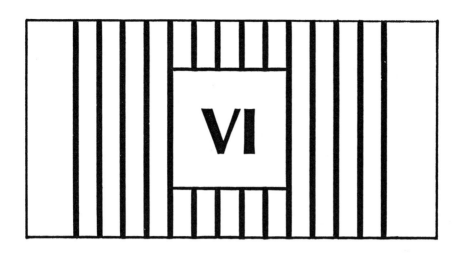

VI

THE PLAYS

THE PLAYS

The plays, with the assignment for each player, are presented with a graphic illustration showing how each play is blocked against each of the three defensive categories: Odd, Even, and Gap.

In order to conserve space, the plays are diagrammed to the right only. To get the assignments for the play going to the left simply mirror each player's assignments.

The plays are presented in the following order:

A. OUTSIDE
1. 121
2. 131
3. 981 OPTION
4. 182 DOWN OPTION
5. NO MO SPR 981 PITCH
6. SPR 121 TRAP OPTION
7. SPR 131 OPTION WALL
8. SPR 991 OPTION
9. 129 TRAP OPTION REV. AT 1

B. CORNER
1. 132
2. 182 DOWN
3. 122 GUT
4. SPR 932 CT XX

C. OFF TACKLE
1. 983
2. 983 X BL
3. NO MO 983 WHAM
4. SPR 123 G.T.
5. SPLIT 933 CT XX
6. SPR 153 DRAW

D. INTERNAL
 1. 134 CT
 2. 134 CT SHORT
 3. 124 G.T.
 4. 924 GUT

E. PASSES
 1. 911
 2. SPR 151
 3. 921 WAGGLE
 4. 161 JET
 5. 121 WAG. HITCH
 6. 181 KP
 7. 981 WAGGLE
 8. SPR 121 TRAP OPTION PASS
 9. 131 KP FLOOD
 10. 134 CT BOOTLEG PASS
 11. SPR 151 SCREEN LH LEFT
 12. 151 CURL AND SCREEN LEFT
 13. 951 HITCH TO FB RIGHT
 14. 129 WAGGLE SHUFFLE AT 2
 15. 129 WAGGLE SCREEN TO FB
 16. SPR 969 SCREEN TO RH LEFT

OUTSIDE PLAY _____ 121 _____
VARIATIONS _____

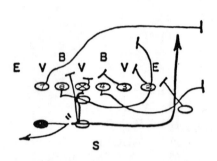

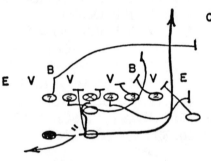

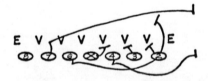

*2–Spread: Crack-Stalk   Split: Down   Tight: Gap-Down-Backer
*3–Gap-Read Up   *(Check W.T. 6 Backer)*
*4–Pull, Block Out on 1st Man Outside of RH's Block
    (Split: 1st Man Outside of End's Block)
*5–Reach-Area
 6–Pull, Wall Off
*7–Cut Off
 8–Spread: Run Out Pattern   Tight: Cut Off
QB–Reverse Pivot, Follow Mid-Line, Handoff to LH, Bootleg at 9
*LH–Carrier, Receive HandofF
*RH–Block First Man Inside
*FB–Dive for Left Foot of 5, Block Area

OUTSIDE

PLAY _____ 131
VARIATIONS _____ SPR 131
131 GAP

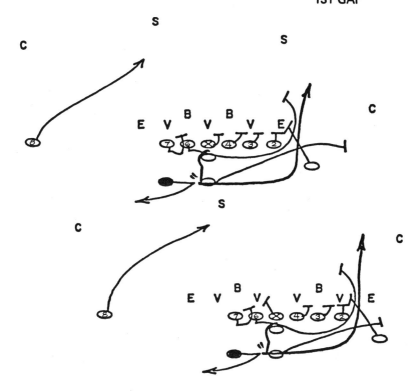

*2–Spread: Crack-Stalk Split: Down Tight: Gap-POST-Read Down
*3–Fire-on-Backer (4 May Gut 3 Single Gap)
*4–Fire-on-Backer (4 May Gut 3 Single Gap)
*5–Fire-on-Backer
*6–Fire-on-Backer (Pull with 6 Call)
*7–Pull Check
 8–Cut Off (Short Yardage or Goal Line, Pull Check)
QB–Reverse Pivot, Follow Mid-Line, Handoff to LH, Bootleg at 9
LH–Carrier
*RH–Block First Man inside
*FB–Take Crossover Step, Block 1st Man Outside of RH'S Block
    Either Way

OUTSIDE

PLAY _____ 981 OPTION _____
VARIATIONS _____ 181 OPTION _____

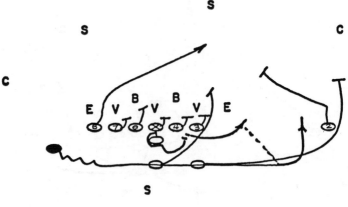

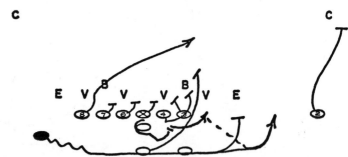

*–Spread: Crack-Stalk   Tight with Wing: Block
 4 Tight Without Wing, Split or Slot: Release, Stalk 5
 3 – Fire-ON-Backer   (Block Down with 4 Call)
 4 – Fire-on-BackeR (Gut with 4 Call)
 5 – Fire-on-Backer
 6 – Fire-on-Backer
 7 – Fire-on-Backer
 8 – Cut Off
 QB – Reverse Pivot, Ride Ball Sharply to FB, Execute Option
 LH – Leave in One Step Motion-Be in Position to Receive Pitch
*RH – Wing: Release Outside of End Man, Stalk 5 Slot or Deep
Back: Flare, Block 4
 FB – Drive for Inside Foot of 2, Turn Up and Block Pursuit

OUTSIDE

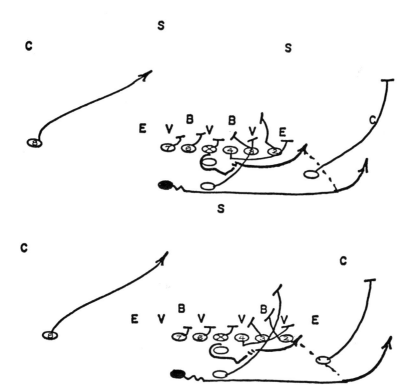

2 – Gap-Read Up
3 – Gap-Down-Backer
4 – Pull-Log 3
5 – Fire-On-Backer
6 – Fire-On-Backer
7 – Fire-On-Backer
8 – Cutoff
QB – Reverse Pivot, Ride Ball Sharply to FB, Execute Option
LH – Leave in One Step Motion. Be in Position to Receive Pitch.
RH – Release Outside-Stalk 5.
FB – Drive for Inside Foot of 2 Turn in and Block 1st Man in Area.

OUTSIDE

PLAY ___ NO MO SPR 981 PITCH ___
VARIATIONS _____

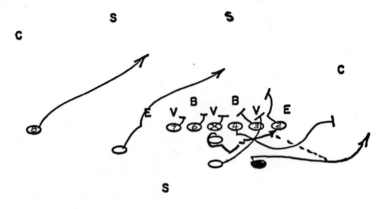

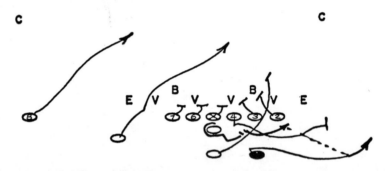

2 – Tight: Gap-Read up   Spread: Crack-Stalk   Split: Down
3 – Gap-Read up
4 – Pull-Block out
5 – Fire-On-Backer
6 – Fire-On-Backer
7 – Fire-On-Backer
8 – Cut OFF
QB – Reverse Pivot-Fake to FB, Option keep or Pitch
LH – Cut off
RH – Shift Weight from Outside Foot to Inside Foot-Flare for
Pittch (Use 36 CT Tech)
FB – Drive for Inside Foot of 2-Turn Up & Block Pursuit

*When wing motion or to a spread, the lead back will block the
first man outside of the tight man.

OUTSIDE

PLAY ___ SPR 121 TRAP OPTION ___

VARIATIONS 121 Trap Option Release

121 TRAP OPTION

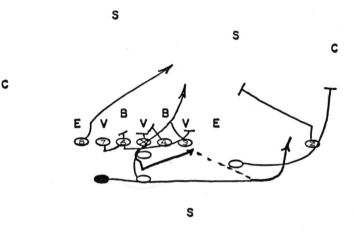

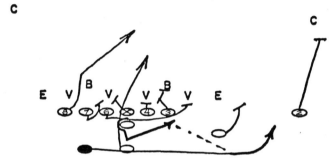

2 – Spread-Crack 4-Stalk 5 (Call 4) Tight, Slot, Split: Release, Stalk 5.

*3 – Gap-Bumplead-Backer

4 – Gap-PosT-Lead-Backer

5 – Post-Left

*6 – Pull, Log 1st Man from Outside Foot of 3

7 – Pull Check

8 – Cutoff

QB – Reverse Pivot to Mid-Line for 2 Steps, option 3

LH – Take Off on Snap, Run Option Path, Look for Pitch

*RH – Check 4-Stalk 5

FB – Fake 24

OUTSIDE

PLAY _____ SPR 131 OPT. WALL _____
VARIATIONS _____

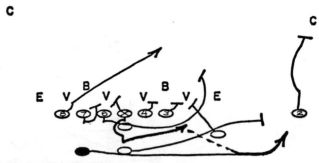

*2 – Tight: Wall Off.   Slot or Split: Release, Stack 5.   Spread: Crack-Stack
*3 – Fire-on-Backer   (4 May Gut 3 Single Gap)
*4 – Fire-on-Backer   (4 May Gut 3 Single Gap)
*5 – Fire-on-Backer
*6 – Fire-on-Backer   (Pull with 6 Call)
*7 – Pull Check
 8 – Cut Off (Short Yardage or Goal Line, Pull Check)
QB – Reverse Pivot to Mid-Line for 2 Steps, Option 3
LH – Take Off on Snap, Run Option Path, Look for Pitch
RH – Prevent Penetration, Wall Off
FB – Flare, Block Support

OUTSIDE   PLAY <u>Spread 991 Option</u>
VARIATIONS <u>RUN to SPR 991 OPT (LOAD)</u>
991 Option PASS

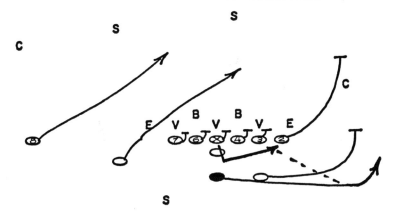

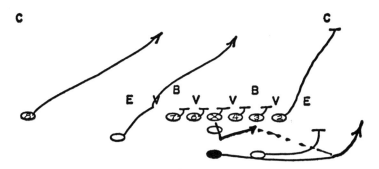

*2 – Spread: Crack-Stalk   Tight: Release, Stalk 5
*3 – Fire-on-Backer
*4 – Fire-on-Backer
*5 – Fire-on-Backer
*6 – Fire-on-Backer
*7 – Fire-on-Backer
 8 – Cutoff
*QB – Take one Step Back, Sprint at 1-Pitch to FB
LH – Cutoff
RH – Flare-Block 4
FB – Carrier: Controlled Sprint at 1-Receive Pitch

OUTSIDE

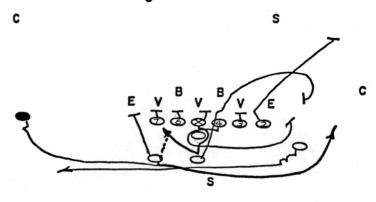

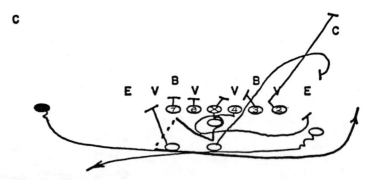

2 – Run Waggle Pattern, Stalk 5
3 – Gap–Down–On
4 – Pull Left Two Steps, Reverse Direction Block at Flank
5 – Fire–On–Backer
6 – Gap–on–Backer
7 – Gap–on–Backer
8 – Carrier: Get Early Depth, Receive Pitch
QB – ReversE Pivot, Fake 129 T. Opt., Pitch to 8
LH – Block 1st Man Outside 7
RH – Fake 29 T. Opt.
FB – Run 29 Waggle, Block at Flank

CORNER

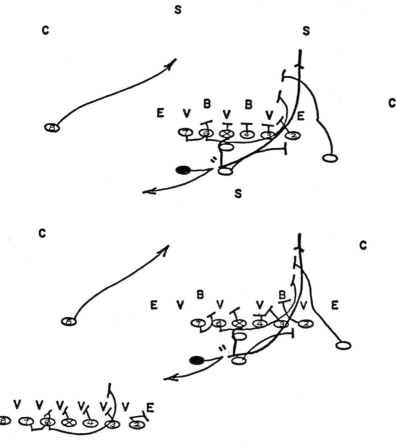

2 – Lead–Backer–Influence   Block Right
*3 – Gap–Post–Lead   (3 Will Call "On," "Short,")
*4 – Gap–Area–Post
*5 – on–Area–Left
*6 – Pull, Wall Off
7 – Pull Check
8 – Cut Off
*QB – Reverse Pivot–Handoff Bootleg at 9
*LH – Carrier: Run Directly for Hole
RH – Influence 1st Man on or Outside of 2, Wall Off
*FB – Head for Tail of 3, Block 1ST Man Outside of 3

CORNER

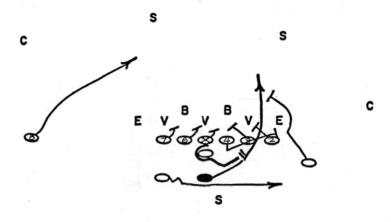

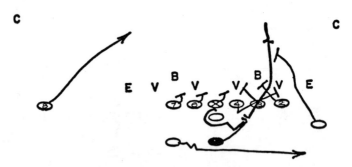

2 – Down–Backer
3 – Gap–Down
4 – Pull–Block Out
5 – Fire–on–Backer
6 – Fire–on–Backer
7 – Fire–on–Backer
8 – Cut Off
QB – Reverse Pivot–Handoff to FB Fake Option
LH – Leave in One Step Motion–Fake Pitch at 1
RH – Influence 1st Man on or Outside of 2–Block Area
FB – Carrier: Run for Inside Foot of 2

CORNER   PLAY ___ 122 GUT ___
                    VARIATIONS ___ 122 ___

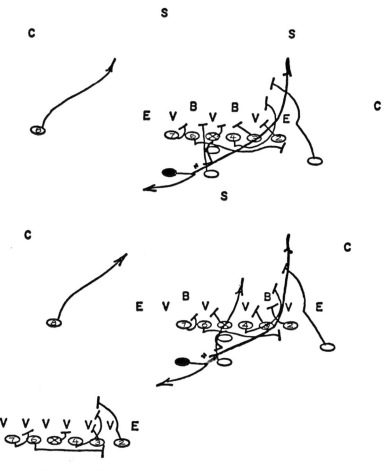

2 – Down–Backer–Influence
3 – Gap–Read Down
4 – Pull–Gut
5 – Reach–Area–Away
6 – Pull–Inside Out
*7 – Gap–Backer–on
8 – Cut Off
QB – Reverse Pivot–Handoff to LH, Bootleg at 9
LH – Carrier: Receive Ball, Cut Inside of 6'S Block
RH – Influence 1st Man on or Outside of 2, Wall Off
FB – Fake 21

CORNER   PLAY ___ SPR 932 CT XX ___
                               VARIATIONS _ T 932 CT XX _

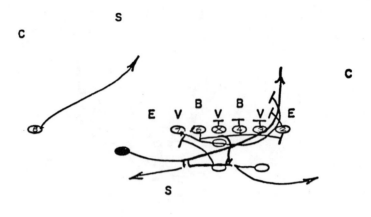

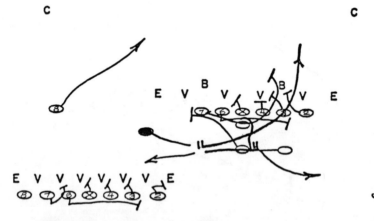

2 – Lead–Backer–Influence–Block Right
3 – Gap–Post–Lead
4 – Gap–Area–Post
5 – on–Area–Left
6 – Pull–Inside Out
7 – Pull Check (Pull-Wall Off Without TE)
8 – Tight: Pull–Wall Off Spread or Slot: Cut Off
QB – Reverse Pivot–Handoff to RH, Bootleg at 1
LH – Carrier: Receive Handoff from RH–Head for Tail of 3
RH – Receive Handoff from QB–Give Ball Inside to LH–Fake at 9
*FB – Dive for Outside Foot of 7, Block 1st Man Off 8'S Tail

OFF-TACKLE PLAY _____ 983 _____

VARIATIONS 983 ON, 143 ON, 983 GUT REL.

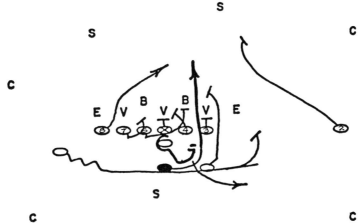

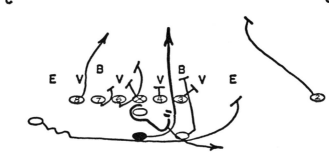

*2 – Tight: on–Outside–Backer   Split: Fake Crackback,
Backer   Spread: Cut Off
3 – On–Outside Gap–Backer
4 – Gap–On–Lead
5 – Post–Left
6 – Pull–Block through the Hole
7 – Pull Check
8 – Cut Off   (X BL vs Single Gap)
QB – Reverse Pivot, Ride Ball to FB, Fake 81 Keep Pass
LH – Leave in Early Motion, Fake 81 Keep Pass
*RH – Step Out–Read Tackle, Block 1st Backer from 5 (Double
Gap–Block 3-4 Seam)
*FB – Carrier: Lead Step, Bend Path for Inside Foot of 3. Read
Defensive Tackle, Select Opening

OFF-TACKLE   PLAY _____ 983 X BL
                        VARIATIONS 936 ct at 3 SPR 936 ct FB at 3

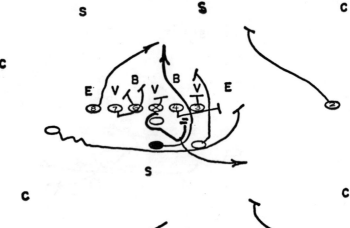

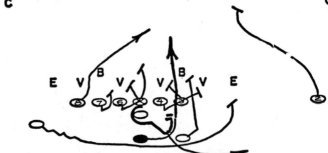

*2 – Tight: Backer Split: Fake Crackback, Backer Spread: Cut Off
 3 – Gap–Down–On
  – Gap–Pull, Block Out (Gap Call)
 5 – On-Left
 6 – Pull-Wall Off Tail of 5
 7 – Pull Check (Odd Block vs. 55)   (Block B vs. 40 Off)
 8 – Cut Off   (Step & Cup vs. 55)
QB – Reverse Pivot, Ride Ball to FB, Fake 81 Keep Pass
LH – Leave in Early Motion, Fake 81 Keep Pass
*RH – Step Out–Dive for 3'S Tail, Block 1st Backer from 5
*FB – Carrier: Lead Step, Bend Path for Inside Foot of 3. Read
Defensive Tackle, Select Opening

OFF-TACKLE

PLAY _____ NO MO 983 WHAM _____

VARIATIONS _____

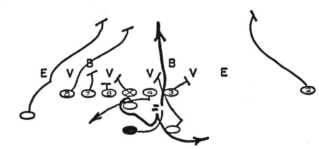

*2 – On-Backer-Outside
 3 – On-Backer-Outside
 4 – Gap-Pull Left
 5 – On-Backer-Left
 6 – On-Backer-Left
 7 – On-Backer
 8 – Cut Off
QB – Reverse Pivot-Ride Ball to FB-Fake 81 Waggle
LH – Cut Off
RH – Dive for 3, 4 Seam-Block Gap, On, Backer
*FB – Carrier: Lead Step, Bend Path for Inside Foot of 3-Read
Area

OFF-TACKLE

PLAY ____ SPR 123 G.T. ____
VARIATIONS 123 G.T. To LH

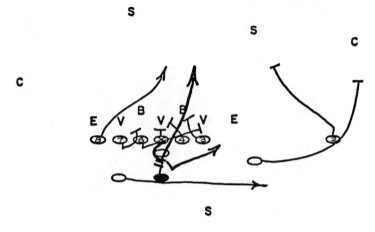

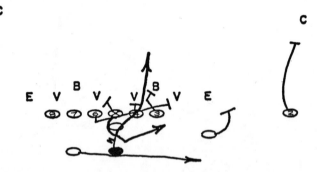

2 – Tight: Gap-On vs. Odd   Backer vs. Even   Spread (Split or Slot): Crack

3 – Bumplead-Backer   (Man in GAP-Backer)   (With TE-Lead-Backer)

4 – Gap-Post-Lead-Backer

5 – Post-Area-Left   (ConditionalPost)

6 – Pull, Inside Out

*7 – Gap-Backer-On

8 – Cut Off

QB – Reverse Pivot, Handoff to FB, Fake Option at 1

LH – Fake 21 Trap Option

RH – Fake 21 Trap Option

*FB – Carrier: Dive for Right Foot of 5

OFF-TACKLE

PLAY _____ Split 933 CT XX _____
VARIATIONS _____ 983 CT _____

2 – Split: Wall Off   Spread: Cut Off
3 – Gap-Lead-Influence, Block Right (Gap StacK-Backer)
4 – Gap-Post-Lead
*5 – Post-Area-Left
6 – Pull-Block Inside Out
*7 – Pull-Check
8 – Pull-Block Through Hole-Wall Off
QB – Reverse Pivot-Handoff to RH, Bootleg at 1
LH – Carrier: Receive Handoff from RH-Head for Tail of 4
RH – Receive Handoff from QB Give Ball Inside to LH Fake AT 9
FB – Dive for Outside Foot of 7, Block 1st Man Off 8'S Tail

Off-TACKLE
PLAY _____ SPR 153 DRAW
VARIATIONS _____

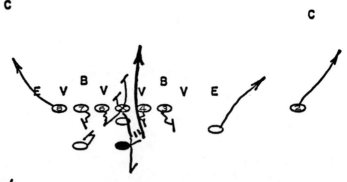

2 – Release
3 – Gap-On-Area-Outside
4 – Gap-On-Area-Delayed Backer
5 – On-Left
6 – Fake Pass Protection-Gut   (Odd Block vs. 55)
7 – On-Outside (Odd Block vs. 55)
8 – Release
QB – Drop Back Behind 4-Give Ball to FB, Continue Fake
LH – Set Up to Block 51-Flare
RH – Release-Block Downfield
FB – Carrier: Step to Side of Play-Accept Ball from QB-Read front

INTERNAL

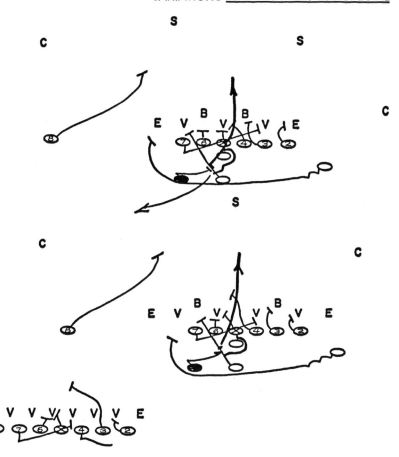

*2 – Gap-On (Backer VS. 40 Off)
*3 – 1st Backer FROM 5-Block Safety
*4 – Gap-Lead-Backer (Influence)
 5 – Post-Lead-Backer
*6 – Area-Post
 7 – Pull, Inside Out
 8 – Cut Off (Go Inside of 3)
*QB – Reverse Pivot, Hand Ball Off to LH, Bootleg at 9
*LH – Carrier: Rock Weight on Left Foot, Receive Inside Handoff
RH – Leave in Early Motion, Block 1st Man Outside of 8
FB – Drive for 6-7 Seam, Block 1st Man in Area

INTERNAL

PLAY _____ 134 CT SHORT _____
VARIATIONS _____

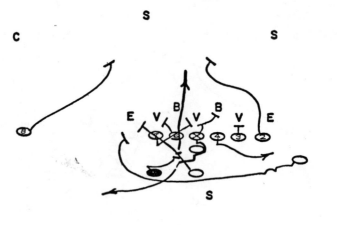

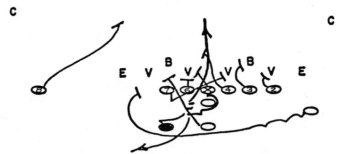

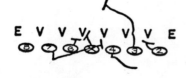

2 – Cutoff
A3 – On-Backer
4 – Pull Away
5 – Fire-Release to Backer
6 – Outside
7 – Pull-Inside Out   (Nose vs. 55)
8 – Cutoff
QB – Reverse Pivot, Hand Ball Off to RH, Bootleg at 9
LH – Carrier: Rock Weight on Left Foot, Receive Inside Handoff
RH – Leave in Early Motion, Block 1st Man Outside of 8
FB – Dive for Inside Foot of 7. Go Off Tail of 7, Block 1st Man in
Area (Backer VS. 55)
With Even Spacing Run Normal Counter or Counter at 8.

INTERNAL   PLAY _____ 124 G.T. _____
                                            VARIATIONS _____

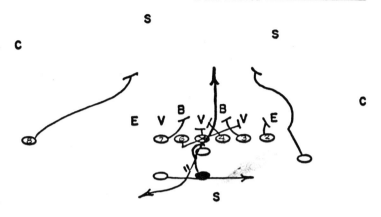

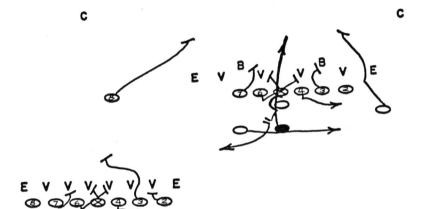

2 – Gap-On
3 – 1ST Backer from 5
4 – Gap-Lead-Backer-Influence
5 – Post-Left
6 – Pull-Inside Out
*7 – Gap-Backer-On
 8 – Gap-On-Backer
*QB – Reverse Pivot, Handoff to FB, Bootleg at 9
LH – Fake 21
RH – Fake 21, Cutoff
*FB – Carrier: Dive for Left Foot of 5

INTERNAL

PLAY ___924 GUT___
VARIATIONS ___924 ON___

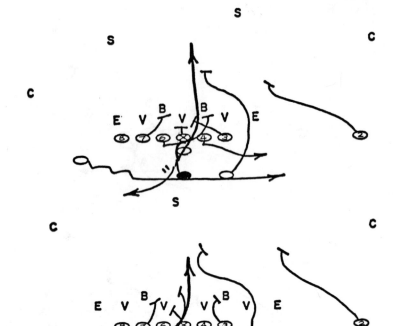

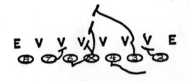

2 – Gap-On (Spread Cutoff)
3 – 1st Backer from 5   (Down to Nose vs. Okla.)
*4 – PULL, Fake 21
5 – Post-Left
6 – PULL, Block Through the Hole
*7 – Gap-Backer-On
8 – Gap-On-Backer
*QB – Reverse Pivot, Handoff to FB, Bootleg at 9
LH – Fake 21
RH – Fake 21, Cut Off
*FB – Carrier: Dive for Left Foot of 5

PASS

PLAY _____ 911
VARIATIONS <u>111 SEAM, 911 THROWBACK</u>

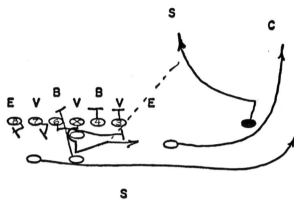

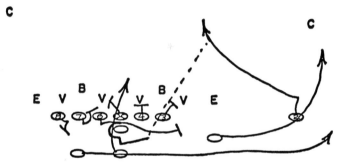

2 – Run "Out" Pattern at 8 Yds.
3 – Fire-On-Area
4 – Fire-On-Area
5 – Step & Cup
6 – Step & Cup
7 – Step & Cup
8 – Crossing Pattern
QB – Sprint Out Right Option Run or Pass
LH – Soft Post
RH – Flat Pattern
FB – Aggressively Block 1st Free Man at Flank

PASS

PLAY _____ SPR 151
VARIATIONS _SPR 951 HOOK_
                951 WEAVE
                151 LH READ

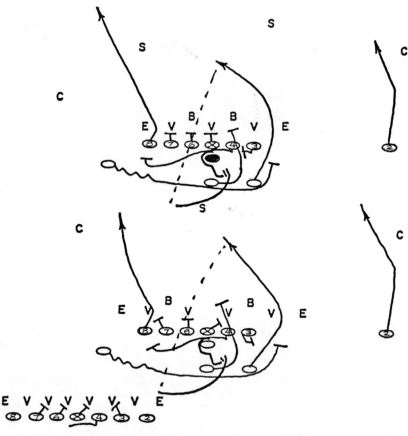

2 – Run "Out" Pattern at 8 Yds
3 – Gap-On-Area-Outside
4 – Gap-on-Area-Outside
5 – Step & Cup

6 – Step & Cup
7 – Step & Cup
8 – Hook at 12 Yds by 7 Yds

QB – Drop Back Right 3-Steps, then to 5-7 Depending on
Development or individual Call
LH – Block 1st Man Outside OF 7'S Block. Release if B Drops &
Hook at 5 Yds in Open Area
RH – Turn Upfield and Look Over Inside Shoulder. (Hook at 12
Yds) Run Companion Route if Pattern is Called
FB – Aggressively Block 1st Free Man-With Called Pattern, Set Up
Behind 4 Man, Fake Draw, Release if Backer Drops. (Check Inside
Backer, Then Outside Backer)

PASS PLAY _____ 921 WAGGLE _____

VARIATIONS 921 WAGGLE OPPOSITE

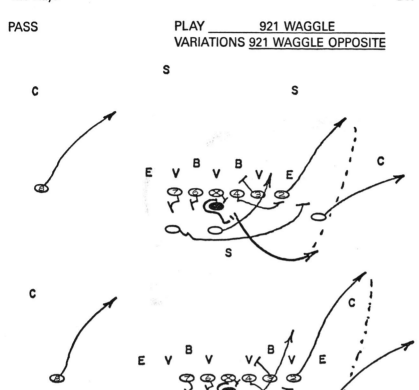

2 – Tight: Crossing Pattern (Read Safety)   Spread:
Post   Pattern-Fake   Middle Safety

3 – Pull Check

4 – Pull-Read 6'S Block, Clean Up Chase, Block Out.   (Do Not
Pull vs. Eagle)

5 – Step & Cup

6 – Pull-Hook 1st Man (Block DE vs 40) from Outside Foot of
TE'S Position

7 – Gap-Down-On

8 – Tight: Waggle Pattern (Release Outside vs.40)   Spread: Fly

QB – Reverse Pivot-Fake to LH-Option Run or Pass

LH – Start in Motion, Block 1st Man Outside of 3'S Block

*RH – Fake 921-Fake Middle Safety-Run Crossing Pattern

FB – Dive for Inside Foot of 6-Block 6'S Area-Slide Delayed into
Flat

PASS

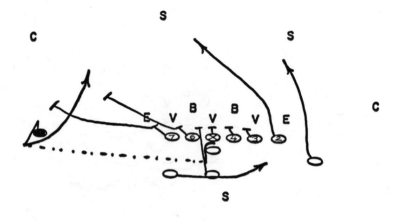

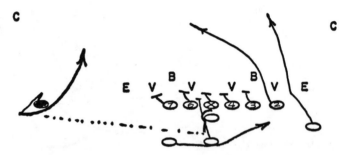

2 – Run Deep Crossing Pattern
3 – Step & Cup
4 – Step & Cup   (Pull vs Even Defense)
5 – Step & Cup
6 – Gap-On-Pull
7 – Gap-On-Outside
8 – Waggle Pattern
QB – Reverse Pivot-Fake to LH-Begin Waggle Path, Set Up on
Inside Foot of 7 at a Depth of 7 Yds
LH – Fake 21, Block 3rd Man-Flare
RH – Fake 21-Run Fly Pattern
FB – Dive for Left Foot of 5, Block Backer

PASS

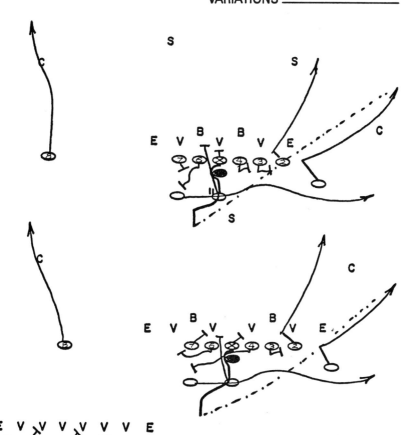

2 – Crossing Pattern-Cut Off
3 – Reach-Cut Off
4 – Reach-Cut Off
5 – Fire-Cut Off
6 – Fire-Release-for Backer
7 – Fire-Release-Block Out
8 – Spread-Run Hitch Pattern Receive Ball, Cut Off 6 & 7
QB – Reverse Pivot-One Step-Pass to 8
LH – Fake 121
RH – Crossing Pattern Cut Off
FB – Dive for Inside Foot of 6

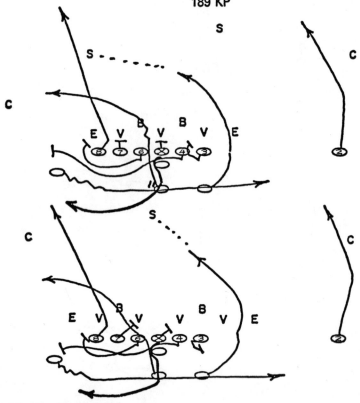

2 – Tight: Seam (Inside Release vs 55)   Spread: Out at 12 Yds
3 – Gap-Down   (With Called Pattern, Gap-On-Area-Outside)
*4 – Pull-Block 1st Man From Outside Foot of TE. (With Called Pattern, Gap-On-Area-Outside)
*5 – Step & Cup
*6 – Step & Cup
*7 – Step & Cup
8 – Step & Cup-Drag   Tight: Crossing
QB – Reverse Pivot-Ride Ball to FB, Option Run or Pass
*LH – One Step Motion-Get in front of QB, Block 1st Man Off Corner
*RH – Sprint to Flat (Look Immediately)
*FB – Straighten Path for Outside Foot of 3, Block 1st Man in Area when Individual Pattern is Called Use 83 Tech

PASS   PLAY _____ 981 WAGGLE _____
                                            VARIATIONS _____

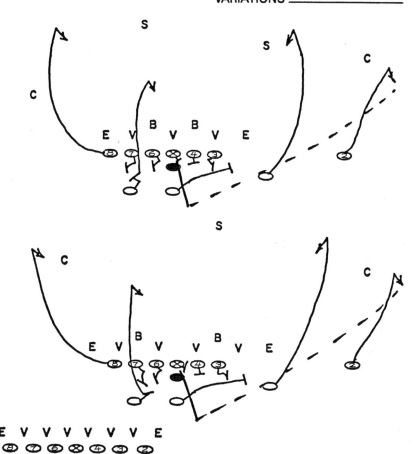

2 – Tight: Crossing Pattern   Spread: Post Pattern
3 – Step & Cup
4 – Pull (Get Depth) Block 1st Man Outside 7'S Block
5 – Step & Cup
6 – Gap-On-Area-Outside
7 – Gap-On-Area-Outside
8 – Waggle Pattern
QB – Reverse Pivot-On Midline-Place Ball on Hip, Get Depth but
do not Threaten Flank
LH – Motion-Block 1st Man Outside OF 3'S Block
RH – Run Crossing Pattern
FB – Take One Lateral Step Right, Bend Path to Block 1st Backer
from 5

PASS

PLAY ___ SPR 121 TRAP OPTION PASS ___
VARIATIONS SPR 121 TRAP OPTION PASS
SLANT & FLY

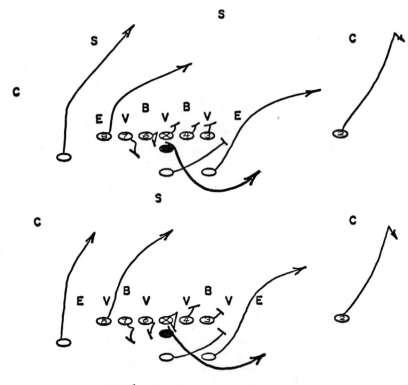

2 – Slant
3 – Gap-On-Area
4 – Gap-On-Area
5 – On-Left
6 – Pull, Block 1st Man Outside 3 (With TE in Pattern Drop)
7 – Step & Cup
8 – Step & Cup
QB – Reverse Pivot to Midline for 2 Steps, Read Secondary, Pass
or Option
*LH – Take Off on Snap, Run Option Path, Look for Pitch-With
Called Pattern, Flare
RH – Flare Outside Slant Pattern, Block
FB – Fake 24 GT-Block 6'S Area

PASS

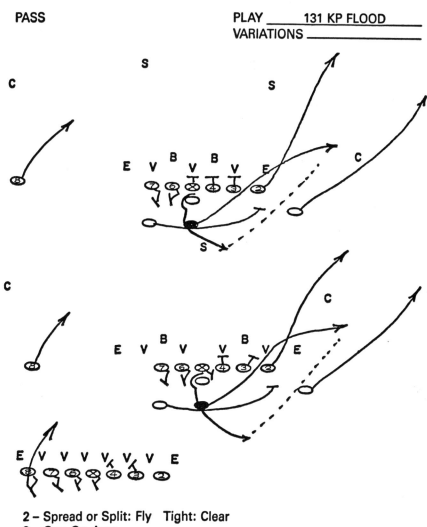

2 – Spread or Split: Fly   Tight: Clear
3 – Gap-On-Area
4 – Gap-On-Area
5 – Step & Cup
6 – Step & Cup
7 – Step & Cup
8 – Step & Cup-Drag
QB – Reverse Pivot-Fake to LH, Set up Behind 3 man to Throw
LH – Fake 31, Block 1st Man Outside of 3 Man
RH – Fly
FB – Dive for Inside Foot of 2, Release Into Flat

PASS

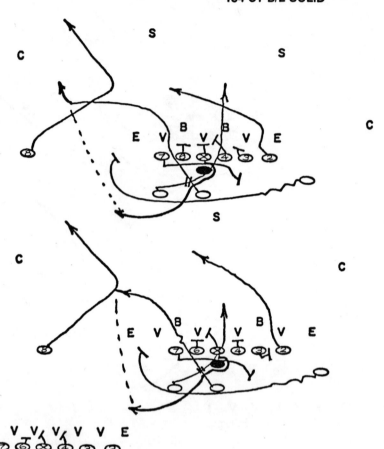

2 – Tight: Crossing Pattern   SpreadL Post
3 – Gap-On-Area-Outside
4 – Gap-On-Lead
5 – Post-Lead
6 – Area-Post
7 – PULL, Block Chase
8 – Angle Flat Pattern-If Covered Sideline at no less than 15 YDS
QB – Reverse Pivot-Fake 34 CT, Bootleg at 9-Run or Pass Option
LH – Fake 34 CT
RH – Leave in Early Motion-Block 1st Free Man Off Corner
FB – Run 34 CT-Run into Flat at 5 Yds
*FB – Block 1st Man Outside 6 When Opposite is Called

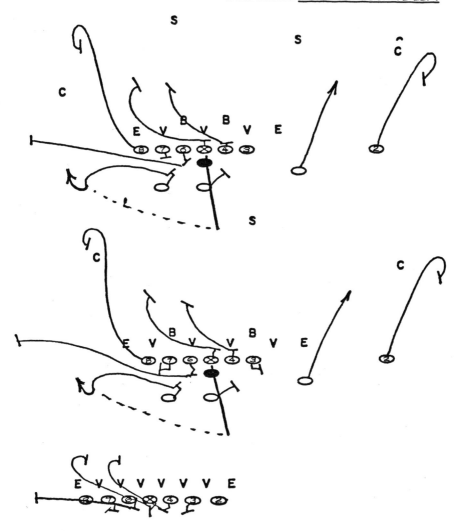

2 – Weave
3 – Gap-On-Area-Cut Off
4 – Gap-On-Area-3 Counts Release Left, Turn In
5 – Step & Cup-3 Counts Release Left-Block Out
*7 – Step & Cup
8 – Tight: Seam-Loop In-Block IN
QB – Sprint Right-Get Depth-Pass to LH
LH – Step Up-Block 1st Man Outside of 7-Release and Receive
Pass
RH – Seam
FB – Step Up, Block Backer

225

PASS   PLAY <u>151 CURL AND SCREEN</u> Left
                                            VARIATIONS _____

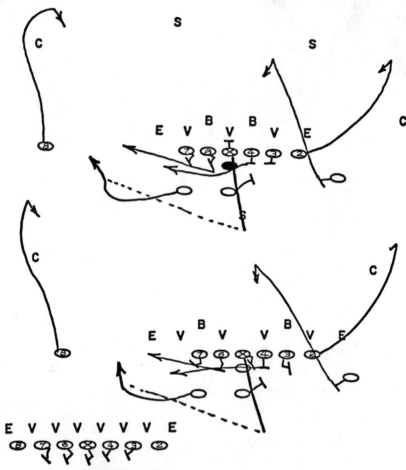

2 – Hook at 12 Yds By 7 Yds
3 – Gap-On-Area-Outside
4 – Gap-On-Area-1 Count Release Left Behind L.O.S.
5 – Step & Cup
6 – Step & Cup-1 Count Release Left Behind L.O.S.
7 – Step and Cup
8 – Curl
QB – Drop Back 7 Steps-Read Hawk
LH – Release Outside, Set Up 7 Yards Wide and 3 Yards Behind
L.O.S.
RH – Step & Cup-Release, Hook at 5 Yards in the Open Area
Between Backers
FB – Set Up Behind 4, Fake Draw. Look for Rush Over 4

PASS

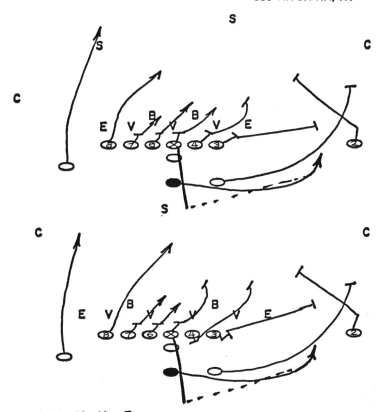

2 – Crack
3 – Fire-Release, Block Out
*4 – Fire-Release for Backer
5 – Fire-Cut Off
6 – Reach-Cut Off
7 – Reach-Cut Off
8 – Crossing Pattern Cut Off
QB – Fake 951 Throw Hitch to FB
LH – Post Pattern
RH – Flare Pattern-Block 5
FB – Fake 51 Block, Flare for Screen

PASS   PLAY <u>129 WAGGLE SHUFFLE AT 2</u>
                                        VARIATIONS _____

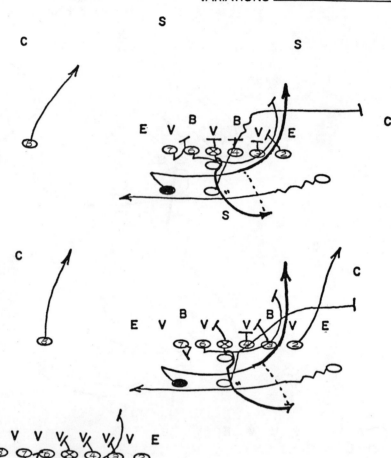

2 – Lead-Man in Gap Release
3 – Gap-Post-Lead
4 – Gap-On-Area
5 – On-Area-Left
6 – Pull Through Hole
7 – Pull Check
8 – Cut Off
QB – Fake 29 Waggle, Shuffle to LH
LH – Fake 29 for 2 Steps, Run for 2-3 Seam, Catch Shuffle
RH – Fake 29 Waggle
FB – – Dive for Inside Foot of 4-Release to Flat and Block 5

PASS

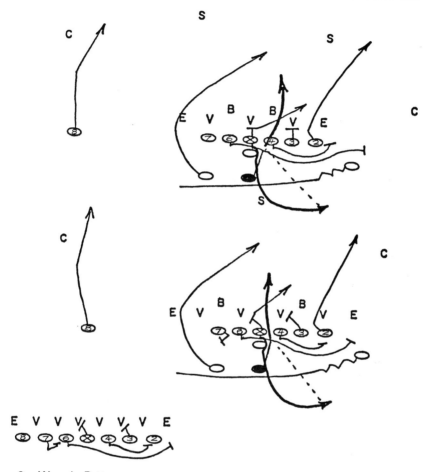

2 – Waggle Pattern
3 – Gap-On-Down   2 Counts-Block Downfield
4 – Pull, Block 1st Man outside of 3
5 – Block 1 Cup-2 Counts Block Downfield
6 – Pull, Block 1st Man Outside of 4's Block
7 – Gap-Backer-On—Away Block Downfield
8 – Post
QB – Reverse Pivot-Fake to RH-Throw Screen to FB
LH – Fake 129-Run Crossing Pattern
RH – Start in Motion-Block Downfield
FB – Dive for Inside Foot of 4, Slide Behind 5'S Block Receive Screen

PASS   PLAY <u>SPR 969 SCR TO RH LEFT</u>
                        VARIATIONS _____

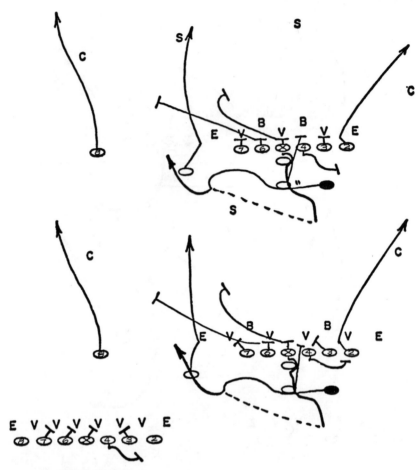

2 – Waggle Pattern
3 – Gap-On-Down
4 – Pull-Block 1st Man Outside of 3
5 – Block 1 Cup-2 Counts Release, Block Back
6 – Gap-On-Area, 2 Counts Release, Block Out
7 – Gap-On-Area
8 – Fly
QB – Reverse Pivot-Fake to RH Begin Waggle Path, Set Up on
Inside Foot of 3 at a Depth of 7 Yards-Throw Screen to RH
LH – Fake 29-Run Fly Pattern
FB – Dive for Right Foot of 5, Block Backer
RH – Fake 29 Block Chase-Receive Screen Pass

BIBLIOGRAPHY

In passing on this "order of football," we are clearly aware of the contributions many coaches have made to the writing of this book and consequently to the evolution of our current Wing-T. Our offense has been one of continual growth that has been inspired by fads of different periods. Football coaches have historically plagiarized ideas from successful systems or formations and much of our innovation has been mutations from other systems.

A review of Delaware Wing-T literature reveals Dave Nelson's (7), statement that the Wing-T of the 1950s was plagiarized 80 percent from the single wing and 20 percent from current T formation teams. I am certain that this modest comment belies his creative thinking. His reasons for using the Wing-T, the advantages of basic formations and philosophy outlined in his book with Evasheski (2) are still the basis of our thinking and are paraphrased again in this book. His presentation at the Ohio State Clinic (20) was an exceptionally clear philosophical outline.

There has been a great deal of writing about individual techniques especially among those coaches who have been a part of our Delaware Staff. Individual techniques have long been a favorite topic in our staff room and each summer we present an in-house clinic. The purpose of this clinic is not only the obvious but an effort to establish a uniform teaching language so that all of our coaches are on the same page with identical coaching phrases. Fritz Crisler (1) described the lead-post principle in his book in 1949. Mike Lude presented our line techniques in 1953 (8). Ed Maley (10) initiated a modern interpretation in 1964 with a classic technique presentation of line techniques. Irv Wisnewski in collaboration with Bill Hunstock (28) wrote an excellent offensive line play article in 1978. I am certain that our line play chapter will reflect a contribution from all of these fine coaches.

Backfield techniques and the Wing-T in general have long been an attractive writing subject. Raymond (9) wrote backfield technique of the Wing-T in 1960. Dunlap (14), Perry (36), and Sabol (39) are but a few of the many coaches who have all written Wing-T articles. Kempski has probably been the most prolific of these writers in recent years (6), (7), (26), (27). Here too the reader will recognize similarities in phrases and writing. We hope you will enjoy the book and use it as a platform from which creative thinking may flow!

Listed below is a bibliography arranged numerically so that you may refer to the above mentioned contributions:

Textbooks

1. Crisler, H.D. Fritz,
   Modern Football,
   McGraw Hill Book Company, New York (1949)

2. Evashevski, Forest and David M. Nelson
   Scoring Power With the Winged-T Offense,
   Wm. C. Brown Company, Dubuque, Iowa (1957)

3. Dietzel, Paul F.
   Wing-T and The Chinese Bandits,
   Chinese Bandits, Baton Rouge, LA (1958)

4. Nelson, David M. and Forest Evashevski,
   The Modern Winged-T Playbook
   Wm. C. Brown Book Company, Dubuque, Iowa (1961)

5. Nelson, David, M.
   Football Principles and Play,
   The Ronald Press Company, New York (1962)

6. Athletic Journal Encyclopedia of Football
   a. The Delaware Wing-T
      Kempski, Ted
   b. Wing-T Options
      Raymond, H.R.
      Parker Publishing Co. Inc.
      West Nyack, NY 1978

Articles from A.F.C.A. Manuals

7. Nelson, David M.
   The Delaware Wing-T Offense,
   A.F.C.A. Proceedings (1957)

8. Lude, Milo
   Offensive Line Play in the Delaware Wing-T,
   A.F.C.A. Proceedings (1958)

9. Nelson, David M. and H.R. Raymond
   Variations of Wing-T Offense
   A.F.C.A. Proceedings (1960).

10. Nelson, David M., H.R. Raymond and E.F. Maley
    Updating the Delaware Wing-T,
    A.F.C.A. Proceedings (1964).

11. Raymond, H.R.
    Backfield Techniques,
    A.F.C.A. Proceeding (1966)

12. Raymond, H. R.
    Delaware's Rushing Game,
    A.F.C.A. Proceedings (1972)

13. Raymond, H.R.
    The Modern Wing-T,
    A.F.C.A. Proceedings (1975)

14. Dunlap, Fred
    What Motivates Use of Wing-T,
    A.F.C.A. Proceedings (1977)

15. Heinecken, Mickey
    Complementing the Wing-T Rushing Attack with Action Passes,
    A.F.C.A. Summer Manual (1977)

16. Raymond, H. R. and T.C. Kempski
    Facelifting the Wing-T,
    A.F.C.A. Proceedings (1979)

17. Kempski, T.C., Chris Raymond, and R. Rogerson
    The Delaware Wing-T Airborne,
    A.F.C.A. Summer Manual (1979)

18. Raymond, H.R.
    Package Football From the Wing-T,
    A.F.C.A. Summer Manual (1982)

19. Rogerson, R.
    The Maine Black Bears Take to the Air,
    A.F.C.A. Summer Manual (1983)

Articles from Other Publications

20. Nelson, David, M.
    The Delaware Wing-T
    Ohio State Football Clinic May 3, 4, 1957

21. Nelson, David, M.
    The Delaware Wing-T,
    Wisconsin High School Coaches Association
    Summer Clinic Aug. 12-16, 1957

22. Nelson, David, M.
    The Delaware Wing-T,
    Football: Texas High School Coaches Association
    Textbook Vol. XX (1958)

23. Nelson, David M.
    The Delaware Wing-T,
    Arizona State University Fifth Annual Football
    Coaches Clinic March 19, 1960

24. Nelson, David M.
    The Delaware Wing-T,
    Twenty Eighth Annual Purdue Football Clinic
    April 8-9, 1960

25. Nelson, David M.
    The Delaware Wing-T,
    Washington State High School Coaches Association (1962)

26. Kempski, Ted
    The Delaware Buck Sweep
    Scholastic Coach, May, June 1975

27. Kempski, Ted
    Belly Series in the Delaware Wing-T
    Athletic, Journal Sept. 1976

28. Wisniewski, Irv and Wm. Hunstock
    Blocking Techniques in the Delaware Wing-T
    Athletic Journal Sept. 1976

29. Purzycki, Joe and Jim Brooks,
    Unbalanced Look in the Wing-T,
    Athletic Journal 58:30 113-116 April, 1978

30. Sprague, Dale L.
    Belly Option Series From Wing-T,
    Scholastic Coach 48:29 52-56 August, 1978

31. Lapinski, Thomas
    The Cross Block,
    Athletic Journal 59:62 98 Sept., 1978

32. Raymond, H.R. and Ted Kempski
    The Delaware Wing-T Offense,
    Kellog Coach of Year Manual

33. Sprice, Gary
   Wing-T Tackle Trap,
   Athletic Journal 59:18 51 April, 1979

34. Dunlap, Fred
   The Wings in Colgates Wing-T,
   Scholastic Coach 48:26-28 June 1979

35. Elias, Wm.
   Wing-T Trap Option,
   Scholastic Coach 3:21 Sept., 1979

36. Perry, Gregg
   Spread Trap Option and Complements from Delaware Wing-T,
   Scholastic Coach 50:24-25 May, June, 1980

37. Raymond, H.R.
   The Wing-T: A System of Moving the Ball,
   Texas Coach 24:22-25-41 Sept., 1980

38. Perry, Gregg and Stephen Verbit,
   Base Backfield Drills - Delaware Wing-T,
   Scholastic Coach 51:68 70 Aug., 1981

39. Sabol, Robert
   Rejuvenating the Traditional Wing-T Flank Game,
   Scholastic Coach 52:60 34 Aug., 1982

40. Smolyn, Donald
   The Delaware Bootleg,
   Coaches Clinic 21:8-11, Sept., 1982

41. Dyer, Peter
   Triple Optioning the Delaware Wing-T,
   Scholastic Coach 51:38 Nov., 1982

42. Sabol, Robert
   Multiple Use of the Delaware Waggle,
   The Coaching Clinic May, 1983

43. Perry, Gregg and Robert Sabol
   Attacking the Split-6 - 8 Man Front,
   Athletic Journal Nov. 1984

44. Raymond, Tubby
   Updating the Delaware Wing-T,
   Champion Coach of the Year Clinics
   Football Clinic Manual, 1985

INDEX

B

Backfield series, 77-79
Ball control:
  the running game and, 27
  the passing game and, 28
Belly series, 79
  cross block and the, 5
  options, 7, 20, 26, 45, 85
  uses of the, 20, 46, 48, 55
Blocking:
  area, 101, 139
  away, 101
  basic scheme for Wing-T, 21
  bumplead, 101, 139
  by the center, 133-135, 136-147
  check, 101, 140
  combination, 137
  crack, 42, 46, 86, 102, 149
  cross block, 5
  cutoff, 102, 140
  double-team trap, 52
  down, 102, 141
  drills for, 145-147
  fire, 102, 141
  by the fullback, 29, 48, 82, 116-117
  gap, 102, 142
  by the guard(s), 48, 78, 82, 94, 96, 97,
    109, 133-135, 136-147
  gut, 102, 142
  by the halfback, 28, 45, 82, 85, 86,
    116-117, 118, 124-126, 128,
    149-150
  individual techniques for, 136, 139-144
  inside-out (trap), 102, 142-143
  J-gut, 102
  lead, 102
  lead-post, 143
  loan, 102
  log, 102, 144
  odd, 102

Blocking *(cont'd)*
  off-tackle, 7, 89, 90, 92
  one-on-one, 52
  for options, 85
  pass, 96, 97, 99, 138
  post, 102
  post-lead, 103
  pull check, 103
  reach, 103, 144
  read up, 103
  schemes for, 21, 80, 82
  shadow, 103
  shoulder, 133-135
  by the split end, 42, 46, 82, 85, 86, 89,
    148-150
  stalk, 149-150
  for the sweep, 3-4
  by the tackle(s), 25, 48, 95, 96, 122,
    125, 133-135, 136-147
  takeoff for, 135-136
  by the tight end, 3, 4, 25, 43, 53, 82,
    86, 89, 128, 148-150
  for the trap option, 7
  up the middle, 94-95
  wall off, 103
  by the wingback, 3-4, 28, 43, 82, 95,
    116-117
Bootleg, 43, 65, 82, 86, 89
  definition of, 99, 101
  see also Waggle

C

Center, the:
  alignment of, 69
  as a blocker, 133-135, 136-147
  drills for, 111-112, 145-147
  snap of the ball and, 81, 106-107
  stance of, 133
  takeoff of, 135-136

D

Defenses:
  attacking, 41-65
  categories of, 32
  combination, 32, 37
  four-deep, 32, 33, 35-37, 42-48, 57-61
  man, 32, 37, 43, 57, 58, 59
  mirror men in, 32, 56, 57
  numbering of men in, 32
  passing against, 55-65
  reading, 32, 43, 100, 108, 109, 110, 130
  secondary coverage, 32, 35-39
  spacing of, 32
  three-deep, 32, 33, 37-39, 49-55, 61-65
  unbalanced, 32
  zone, 32, 33, 35-36, 37-39, 57-65
Diveback. *see* Halfback, the

E

Ends. *see* Split end, the; Tight end, the

F

Four-deep defenses:
  adjustments of, 35-37
  attacking the flank of, 42-46
  attacking the middle of, 47-48
  attacking off tackle against, 46-47
  description of, 32, 33, 35
  passing against, 57-61
Fullback, the:
  alignment of, 69, 70, 73
  as a ball carrier, 5, 21, 26, 28-29,
       49-50, 52-54, 77, 78, 79, 108, 110,
       126, 128, 131-132
  as a blocker, 29, 48, 82, 116-117
  drills for, 111-112, 115, 131-132
  handoff and, 118, 126, 128
  motion and, 76
  options and, 26
  as a receiver, 29, 44, 58, 60, 80, 97,
       109
  role of, in the Wing-T, 21, 28-29
  stance of, 116
  takeoff of, 117
  the waggle and, 5
Full T, weakness of the, 19

G

Guard(s), the:
  alignment of, 69

Guard(s), the *(cont'd)*
  as a blocker, 48, 78, 82, 94, 96, 97,
       109, 133-135, 136-147
  drills for, 145-147
  the sweep and, 4
  takeoff of, 135-136
  the trap and, 7
  the waggle and, 5

H

Halfback, the:
  alignment of, 69, 70, 73
  as a ball carrier, 7, 23, 28, 45, 47,
       51-52, 77, 78, 108, 110, 118-123,
       131-132
  as a blocker, 28, 45, 82, 85, 86,
       116-117, 118, 124-126, 128,
       149-150
  drills for, 111-112, 114-115, 131-132
  handoff and, 117-118, 119, 121, 122
  motion and, 23, 74-76
  as a receiver, 28, 62, 80, 100, 129-130
  role of, in the Wing-T, 28
  stance of, 116
  takeoff of, 117
  the trap and, 7
  see also Wingback, the
Horizontal stretch, 55, 58

I

I Formation:
  position of running backs in the, 69
  weakness of the, 19

K

Keep pass(es), 46, 50, 65, 96
  definition of, 102

L

Lead option, 85
Linemen, offensive, *see* under names of
  individual positions, e.g.,
  Guard(s), the

M

Man defensive coverage, 32, 37
  passing against, 43, 57, 58, 59
Mirror men, 32, 56, 57
Misdirection. *see* Motion
Motion, 92, 97
  extended, 74-76, 81

Motion *(cont'd)*
  the fullback and, 76
  the halfback and, 23, 74-76
  the quarterback and, 23
  the split end and, 75, 76
  as a strength of the Wing-T, 21
  the tight end and, 45, 46, 75, 76
  the wingback and, 23, 28, 74, 75-76, 89
  where to run, 46
Motivation:
  definition of, 8
  negative, 8-9
  pep talks, 16-18
  player "ownership" of the team, 14-15
  positive, 9
  self-esteem, 15-16
  setting goals, 16

O

Offense:
  alignment, 69
  backfield series, 76-79
  cadence, 81
  down and distance, 182
  down requirements and suggested calls, 182-183
  field position, 180-182
  formations, 70-76
  game plan, 184
  inside (up-the-middle) game, 94-95
  numbering system, 68-81, 82
  off-tackle game, 89-90, 92
  outside game, 82, 85-86, 89
  points of attack, 80, 82
  sample teaching progression, 166-170
  score, 178-179
  starting signal, 81
  time, 179-180
  use of personnel, 184
  wind and weather, 183-184
Offensive linemen. *see* under names of individual positions, e.g., Guard(s), the
Option(s):
  belly, 7, 20, 26, 45, 85, 110
  blocking for, 85
  definition of, 102
  fullback, 26
  lead, 85
  quarterback, 26, 43-44, 79, 85, 86, 109, 110-111

Option(s) *(cont'd)*
  trap, 5, 7, 45, 85
  trap option pass, 46, 60-61, 110-111
  triple, 26
  wall, 85
Orientation, sample summer letters for, 10-14

P

Passing game, the:
  against four-deep defenses, 57-61
  against mirror men, 32, 56, 57
  against three-deep defenses, 61-65
  balance of, 27-28
  ball control and, 28
  categories of, 57, 95
  controlling the defense with, 55
  the fullback and, 29, 44, 58, 60, 80, 97, 109
  getting a receiver open, 56-57
  the halfback and, 28, 62, 80, 100, 129-130
  horizontal stretch, 55, 58
  keep passes, 46, 50, 65, 96, 102
  play-action, 19-20, 26, 28, 42, 50, 60-61, 64
  the quarterback and, 5, 23, 26, 29, 32, 43-44, 65, 77, 78, 79, 80, 81, 82, 85, 86, 89, 96, 97, 99-100, 102, 106-115, 117-118, 130
  screen passes, 59
  the split end and, 27, 38, 39, 42, 46, 50, 51, 56, 57, 62, 64, 80, 86, 97, 100, 150-163
  the tight end and, 46, 58, 80, 86, 100, 109, 150-163
  trap option pass, 46, 60-61
  vertical stretch, 55, 60, 65
  waggle passes, 50
  the wingback and, 28
  see also Blocking
Play-action passes, 19-20, 26, 28
  types of, 50
  when to use, 42, 60-61, 64
Plays:
  24, 94
  24 Guard Trap, 94
  24 Gut, 94
  24 On, 94
  80 Down Option, 49
  80 Keep Pass, 97

Plays *(cont'd)*
80 No Mo pitch, 46
80 Waggle, 97
82 Down, 112
90 Option, 46
111 Seam, 215
121, 3-4, 53, 82, 118, 119, 124, 192
121 Release, 43
121 Trap Option, 197
121 Trap Option Release, 197
121 Wag Hitch, 219
122, 203
122 Gut, 53, 90, 121, 203
123 Guard Trap, 126, 128
123 Guard Trap to Left Halfback, 7, 92,
    121-122, 208
124, 109
124 Guard Trap, 109, 126, 213
124 Gut, 109, 126
124 On, 109, 126
129, 4
129 Trap Option, 5, 7
129 Trap Option Reverse at 1, 200
129 Waggle, 5
129 Waggle Screen to Fullback, 229
129 Waggle Shuffle at 2, 228
131, 82, 125, 193
131 Gap, 193
131 Keep Pass Flood, 223
132, 90, 121, 201
132 Gap, 201
134 Counter, 4, 95, 110, 122, 123, 211
134 Counter Bootleg Pass, 224
134 Counter Bootleg Solid, 224
134 Counter Gut, 95, 211
134 Counter Short, 95, 212
134 Counter Special, 211
137 Counter XX, 92
142 Down, 202
142 Down Option, 195
143 On, 205
151 Curl and Screen Left, 226
151 Left Halfback Read, 216
161 In, 218
161 Jet, 218
181 Keep Pass, 220
181 Keep Pass Opposite, 220
181 Option, 194
182 Down, 43, 90, 110, 128, 202
182 Down Option, 7, 43, 82, 119, 120,
    195

Plays *(cont'd)*
182 Gut, 128, 202
187, 92
187 Cross Block, 5, 92
187 Gut, 92
189 Keep Pass, 220
189 Option, 112
199 Option, 112
911, 215
911 Throwback, 215
921, 85, 119, 124-125, 126
921 Trap Option, 110-111, 120
921 Waggle, 217
921 Waggle Opposite, 217
924 Gut, 214
924 On, 214
929 Bootleg, 89
929 Waggle, 89
933 Counter Criss Cross, 122
934 Counter, 123
936 Counter at 3, 206
936 Counter Bootleg, 89
951 Curl, 100
951 Hitch to Fullback Right, 227
951 Weave, 216
961 Curl, 218
981 Keep Pass, 110
981 Option, 110, 112, 125, 194
981 Option Load, 120, 126
981 Waggle, 221
983, 205
983 Counter, 209
983 Cross Block, 128, 206
983 Gut Rel., 205
983 On, 205
989 Hitch to Right Halfback Right, 227
991 Option, 112, 128
BL 51 Hitch to Right Halfback, 227
No Mo 983 Wham, 207
No Mo Spread 981 Pitch, 196
Right 121, 85
Right 931, 85
Run to Blue 51 Post, Fly and Flat, 100
Split 931, 85
Split 933 Counter XX, 209
Spread 121, 82
Spread 121 Trap Option, 111-112, 120,
    126, 197
Spread 121 Trap Option Pass, 222
Spread 121 Trap Option Pass Slant &
    Fly, 222

Plays *(cont'd)*
   Spread 123 Guard Trap, 208
   Spread 123 Gut Guard Trap, 92
   Spread 131, 82, 193
   Spread 132, 201
   Spread 134 Counter Bootleg Opposite,
     224
   Spread 151, 100, 216
   Spread 151 Screen Left Halfback Left,
     225
   Spread 153 Draw, 210
   Spread 181 Keep Pass (Called Pattern),
     220
   Spread 181 Keep Pass Screen Tight End
     Left, 225
   Spread 921, 82
   Spread 929 Trap Option, 111-112
   Spread 929 Waggle, 89
   Spread 929 Wag Shuffle, 90
   Spread 932 Counter XX, 90, 204
   Spread 936 Counter, 90
   Spread 936 Counter at 2, 201
   Spread 939 Counter Fullback at 3, 206
   Spread 951 Hook, 216
   Spread 969 Screen to Right Halfback
     Left, 230
   Spread No Mo 981 Keep Pass, 220
   T 132 Counter XX, 204
   Z 82 Down, 47
   Z 132, 201
   Z 182 Down, 202
Practice:
   Friday's, 173
   importance of, 171-172
   Monday's, 172
   sample schedule for, 173-177
   Sunday's, 172
   Thurday's, 173
   Tuesday's, 172-173
   Wednesday's, 173
Pro formations, weakness of, 19

Q

Quarterback, the, 80, 96, 97, 108-111
   as a ball carrier, 45-46, 109
   the bootleg and, 43, 65, 82, 86, 89, 99
   cadence and, 81
   drills for, 111-115
   dropback of, 78, 99-100, 102, 107-108
   handoff of, 117-118
   motion and, 23

Quarterback, the *(cont'd)*
   options and, 26, 43-44, 79, 85, 86, 109
   reading defenses, 32, 43, 100, 108, 109,
     110, 130
   role of, in the Wing-T, 29
   setup of, 78
   snap of the ball and, 81, 106-107
   the sprint out and, 77, 96
   stance of, 106
   starting signal and, 81
   the waggle and, 5, 82, 86, 89, 99, 108,
     109

R

Receivers. *see* under name of position,
   e.g., Tight end, the
Running backs. *see* under name of
   position, e.g., Fullback, the
Running game, the:
   advantages of, 27
   ball control and, 27
   the fullback and, 5, 21, 26, 28-29,
     49-50, 52-54, 77, 78, 79, 108, 110,
     126, 128, 131-132
   the halfback and, 7, 23, 28, 45, 47,
     51-52, 77, 78, 108, 110, 118-123,
     131-132
   the quarterback and, 45-46, 109
   the split end and, 45
   the tight end and, 43
   the wingback and, 43
   see also Blocking

S

Single-back offense, weakness of the, 19
Split end, the:
   alignment of, 69, 71, 72, 73, 74
   as a ball carrier, 45
   as a blocker, 42, 46, 82, 85, 86, 89,
     148-150
   drills for, 114, 161-163
   motion and, 75, 76
   positioning of, 49
   as a receiver, 27, 38, 39, 42, 46, 50, 51,
     56, 57, 62, 64, 80, 86, 97, 100,
     150-163
   release of, 150-151
   stance of, 148
   the sweep and the, 4
   the waggle and, 44
Spread end. *see* Split end, the

Sprint out, 77, 96
Sweep, the:
    blocking for, 3-4
    playside guard and, 4
    the split end and, 4
    the tight end and, 3, 4
    wingback and, 3-4

T

Tackle(s), the offensive, 33:
    alignment of, 69
    as a blocker, 25, 48, 95, 96, 122, 125,
        133-135, 136-147
    drills for, 145-147
    takeoff of, 135-136
Tackle trap, 4
Three-deep defenses:
    adjustments of, 37-39
    attacking the flank of, 49-51
    attacking the middle of, 54-55
    attacking off tackle against, 51-54
    description of, 32, 33
    passing against, 61-65
Tight end, the:
    alignment of, 69, 70, 72, 73
    as a ball carrier, 43
    as a blocker, 3, 4, 25, 43, 53, 82, 86,
        89, 128, 148-150
    drills for, 113-115, 161-163
    motion and, 45, 46, 75, 76
    positioning of, 49
    as a receiver, 46, 58, 80, 86, 100, 109,
        150-163
    release of, 150-151
    stance of, 148
    the sweep and the, 3, 4
    the waggle and, 45, 46
Trap(s):
    counter, 20
    guard, 7
    the halfback and, 7
    option, 5, 7, 45, 85
    tackle, 4
Trap option pass, 46, 60-61
Triple option, 26

V

Vertical stretch, 55, 60, 65

W

Waggle, the, 46;
    definition of, 103
    the fullback and, 5
    the guards and, 5
    passes, 50
    the quarterback and, 5, 82, 86, 89, 99,
        108, 109
    the split end and, 44
    the tight end and, 45, 46
    the wingback and, 44
    see also Bootleg
Wide out. see Split end, the
Wingback, the:
    alignment of, 69, 70, 72, 73, 74
    as a ball carrier, 43
    as a blocker, 3-4, 28, 43, 82, 95,
        116-117
    drills for, 112, 113-115
    motion and, 23, 28, 74, 75-76, 89
    as a receiver, 26, 28, 42, 51, 58, 60, 62,
        63, 64, 100
    role of, in the Wing-T, 28
    stance of, 116
    the sweep and the, 3-4
    takeoff of, 117
    the waggle and, 44
    see also Halfback, the
Wing-T, the:
    alignment of, 28
    balanced passing of, 27-28
    basic principles of, 26-27
    blocking, 3, 21
    description of, 19-20
    motion, 21, 23
    options, 5, 20, 26
    play-action passing, 19-20, 26, 28, 60-61
    pressuring the defense, 25-26
    as primarily a running attack, 27
Wishbone, weakness of the, 19

Z

Z attack, 45, 46-47
Zone defensive coverage, 33
    finding an opening in, 56-57
    four-deep, 35-36, 57-61
    mirror men and, 32, 56, 57
    three-deep, 37-39, 61-65